The Presence in the Midst

To Pamela, with love and thankfulness

The Presence in the Midst

reflections on discernment

Peter J Eccles

Swarthmore Lecture 2009

First published July 2009

Quaker Books, Friends House, 173 Euston Road, London NW1 2BJ

www.quaker.org.uk

ISBN 978 1 907123 03 0

Cover design Hoop Associates
Book design and typesetting Golden Cockerel Press Ltd, London
Printed Ashford Colour Press Ltd

The Swarthmore Lecture

The Swarthmore Lectureship was established by the Woodbrooke Extension Committee at a meeting held 9 December 1907: the minute of the Committee providing for an "annual lecture on some subject relating to the message and work of the Society of Friends". The name Swarthmore was chosen in memory of the home of Margaret Fox, which was always open to the earnest seeker after Truth, and from which loving words of sympathy and substantial material help were sent to fellow workers.

The Lectureship continues to be under the care of Woodbrooke Quaker Study Centre trustees, and is a significant part of the education work undertaken at and from Woodbrooke.

The lectureship has a twofold purpose: first, to interpret to the members of the Society of Friends their message and mission; and second, to bring before the public the spirit, aims and fundamental principles of Friends. The lecturers alone are responsible for any opinions expressed.

The lectureship provides both for the publication of a book and for the delivery of a lecture, the latter usually at the time of Britain Yearly Meeting of the Society of Friends. A lecture related to the present book was delivered at Yearly Meeting in York on the evening of Tuesday 28 July 2009.

The Swarthmore Lecture Committee can be contacted via the Clerk, c/o Woodbrooke Quaker Study Centre, 1046 Bristol Road, Selly Oak, Birmingham B29 6LJ.

Woodbrooke
Quaker Study Centre

Thou, Nature, art my goddess; to thy law
My services are bound.

William Shakespeare,
King Lear, Act 1 Scene 2

A motto used by the great mathematician
Carl Friedrich Gauss (1777–1855)

Contents

Introduction & Acknowledgements

By the time this lecture is given it will be over three years since I was first approached about giving a Swarthmore Lecture on the subject of "discernment". This is the third of three successive Swarthmore Lectures given by Friends who have been very active in the central work of our yearly meeting, reflecting on what they have learnt from this experience and from other aspects of their rather different lives. As I listened to and subsequently read the lectures by Beth Allen and Christine Davis, I wondered what there was left for me to say.

Discipleship, stewardship and discernment are closely related, each being aspects of how we live a faithful life. Both Beth Allen who spoke about discipleship and Christine Davis who spoke about stewardship included material on discernment in their lectures, and Beth Allen even included a quote from me which I had already begun to see as the starting point for my lecture (see Beth Allen 2007, pp. 41 and 42, now expanded to the first part of my Chapter 6). In each of our lectures we have felt it necessary to explore our understanding of God and how we experience God at work in the world, but I hope that our different approaches will be helpful.

I am not a scientist, not a philosopher, not a theologian and not a historian. Nevertheless, as I have worked on this lecture I have found myself drawn into areas which require expertise in each of these disciplines. To experts, and probably others, my lack of expertise and indeed of knowledge will be very evident. Much of my knowledge has come from reading some of the popular accounts of these disciplines which seem to appear in ever greater numbers. In particular, the area of the relationship between science and religion is a vast one with an enormous and fascinating literature; from time to time I have become immersed in this rather than working on the lecture.

1

There is probably more discussion of science in this lecture than Friends are used to, but for me the ideas of science are essential in trying to understand the world around us. This picks up a theme from another recent Swarthmore Lecture. Jackie Leach Scully (2002, p. 103) wrote that "without exception each of us is called to understand something of what science says about the world". I would echo that. The scientific method is immensely powerful and has transformed the way that we understand the world. "Scientific investigation of all kinds offers paths into creation that … run parallel to the ones that mystics take, and tend to end up in the same place" (p. 4). I agree that scientific understanding complements the understanding which comes through our spiritual experiences. It is essential to reconcile the two though this is not always easy and may lead us to question some of our religious views. An early Swarthmore lecturer, Silvanus Thompson, who was also a mathematician, wrote that "no thinking [person's] views are worth much until he [or she] has tested them – has gone through the process of looking them in the face and questioning their validity, their authority; until in fact he [or she] has gone through the stage of doubting them, and has passed through the stage of doubt to the fuller experience of conviction" (Silvanus P. Thompson 1915, p. 93).

My ideas have changed and developed in the course of working on this lecture and I have certainly gone through "the stage of doubt" many times. It sometimes seems difficult to get beyond that stage. I am left with as many questions as I began with, but I can testify to the truth of Silvanus Thompson's claim that this questioning can lead to a fuller experience of conviction as for T. S. Eliot in "Little Gidding", where "the end of our exploring / Will be to arrive where we started / And know the place for the first time" (T. S. Eliot, "Little Gidding", V).

This lecture is my attempt to set out where I have reached in my consideration of the fundamental question of existence: how do we make sense of and respond to our experience of the world around us? What I bring to the lecture is 60 years of being a Friend; this has played a large part in shaping who I am. I recognise that any contribution I have made to Friends has been rather by enabling and supporting other Friends with the vision to make a real difference than by being a visionary or activist myself. It has been a real privilege to work with some of these Friends. I have also worked as a mathematician, mainly at the University of Manchester, teaching, learning and occasionally discovering/ creating new mathematics. In that world too I have been an enabler rather than an activist and there too it has been a privilege to work with some wonderful teachers, researchers and scholars. Swarthmore Lectures are normally given by the visionaries or the activists and I am very conscious of the limitations of the experience I bring to the task. I am also aware that the lecture marks for me just the beginning of the exploration of many ideas expressed in it. There are therefore many loose ends and unanswered questions.

I need to mention the thread of music which runs through this lecture. There has always been music. My only real memories of infant school are of singing in the school hall. The first piece of composed music I remember hearing was the third movement *scherzo: vivace* from Antonin Dvořák's Symphony no. 7 in D minor, the signature tune for a serial on "Children's Hour" on the wireless which I looked forward to hearing each week; the piece still gives me a thrill every time I hear it. Since then I have played a little, sung a little and listened a lot. There is a sense in which great music has an eternal existence, out of time – which is paradoxical since it only makes sense as an experience in time. The shared experience of music-making, with each person bringing their own contribution to a whole which is greater than the sum of the parts, is a model for the communal life to which we aspire. I acknowledge within the lecture this importance of music to me by using a number of quotations associated with pieces of music or composers.

In working on this lecture I have been supported by my family, Pamela Eccles, Mark Eccles, Michael Eccles and Heather Rowlands, who all seemed to take for granted that preparing this lecture was something that I could do. The Swarthmore Lecture Committee, and in particular Val Ferguson, Peter Fishpool and Julia Gordon, have been a source of support and encouragement. The Committee appeared to continue to believe throughout that I had something to say, and the criticism of draft texts by the whole group or individual members has been unfailingly constructive and helpful. In the final stages, Deborah Padfield has made numerous suggestions which have helped to make the text less clumsy and incomprehensible, and John Fitzgerald has been overseeing the publication; it has been a pleasure to work with both of them.

I learnt what it was to be a Quaker from my parents, William Eccles and Gladys Eccles, and by growing up with some wonderful Friends in Blackpool Meeting and Preston Monthly Meeting. Since then, the development of my religious faith has been influenced by Friends in Cambridge and in Young Friends Central Committee, by many Friends encountered through regular attendance at Yearly Meeting, and by long involvements in Meeting for Sufferings, Friends World Committee for Consultation and the Leaveners, and most of all by building a life together with Pam. For nearly 40 years, our local meeting at Cheadle Hulme has provided a spiritual home, and was our actual home for the five years when we lived at the meeting house. Friends there, and more widely in Cheshire – now East Cheshire – have always been a source of support. I have been very fortunate.

Peter J. Eccles
Manchester, June 2009

CHAPTER 1

The Presence in the Midst

S itting in meeting for worship, everything seems still.
Outside the world goes on. We may hear sounds of
human activity: the voices of passers by and the sounds of traffic.
We may hear the sounds of the natural world: sometimes birds
singing, sometimes the wind and the rain beating against the
windows. We may be aware that the earth is not really still but is
turning on its axis and travelling along its orbit round the sun.

Here it is still, but elsewhere the earth is teeming with activity:
people are being born, people are dying, people are in pain,
people are joyful, people are doing dreadful things, people are
doing wonderful things.

We seek to still our thoughts.

But our brains are still active, ensuring that we continue to
breathe and to sit upright, processing information received from
the outside world, through our eyes, our ears, our sense of touch,
our sense of smell, even our taste buds.

And yet our minds do know stillness. We find ourselves
"[a]t the still point of the turning world. / …at the still point,
there the dance is, / But neither arrest nor movement" (T. S. Eliot,
"Burnt Norton" II).

This is the heart of the Quaker experience for us: to know
stillness, sensing the eternal, and at the same time to be aware
of the dance, the teeming activity around us. In this shared
experience we "enter…into the joys and sorrows of each other's

lives" (*Advices & Queries* §18), and at the same time can also be aware of the joys and sorrows of the whole of humanity, of the joy and sorrow of the whole of creation. A gathered meeting is the still centre of the whole universe, a moment when time stands still and we are in touch with eternity.

This experience is not of course uniquely Quaker. The author of Psalm 46 wrote the familiar words

> Be still, and know that I am God.

These words, from the Authorised Version, have been set to music by David Saunders and by Ian Smale (*Sing in the Spirit* 2005, 68 and 70). They are echoed in Britain Yearly Meeting's current *Advices & Queries*:

> We seek a gathered stillness in our meetings for worship so that all may feel the power of God's love drawing us together and leading us (*Advices & Queries* §8).

What does "stillness" mean? A more modern translation of the psalm may be helpful – this is the New English Bible:

> Let be then; learn that I am God.

So to "be still" is to "let be", to accept. I have always preferred the word "stillness" to "silence". Silence can seem dead and empty whereas stillness feels rich with possibilities.

To be still or to accept can be difficult in a world where we know there is so much pain and suffering, some of it caused by human beings' actions towards each other, but much of it caused by the very nature of the creation. But the psalmist and our own *Advices & Queries* tell us that if we are still or if we do "let be" then we will know God, we will "feel the power of God's love drawing us together and leading us". This experience, how we use it to make sense of our lives, and as a guide to how we live our lives, is the subject of this lecture.

The title of the lecture comes from the well-known 1916

painting by James Doyle Penrose, *The Presence in the Midst,* which pictures a meeting for worship of earlier years taking place in Jordans Meeting House, with Jesus, the Christ, standing in the meeting.[1] This reflects an understanding that the experience of meeting for worship is an encounter with Christ, identified with the historic person of Jesus of Nazareth. Today some Friends may need to find other words and images to convey their understanding of this experience.

1.1 God language

Talking about our deepest experiences is difficult since we struggle to find a shared vocabulary with which we are comfortable. We may feel hesitant about the use of the word "God" partly because we are uncomfortable with the way that others use the word. However, we *do* use this word, and if for example we look at Britain Yearly Meeting's current *Advices & Queries* we find the following phrases:

> "the leadings of God" (§1)
> "God's love" (§2, §8, §11, §18, §29)
> "God's guidance" (§3, §9, §14, §25, §27, §28)
> "obedience to God" (§4)
> "the spirit of God at work ... in your daily life" (§7)
> "God's presence" (§8, §12, §26)
> "God's purposes" (§35)
> "God's continuing creation" (§42)

All of these phrases require some interpretation.

The word "Christ" may be more difficult and now appears less often in British Quaker writings. In the current *Advices & Queries* the word is only used twice:

> Bring the whole of your life under the ordering of the spirit of Christ (§2)

and a special case of this:

> Do you faithfully maintain our testimony that war and
> the preparation for war are inconsistent with the spirit
> of Christ? (§31)

We may now use the word "Christ" less often but this does
not mean that the experience captured by the word is any less
powerful for us. The advice to "bring the whole of your life under
the ordering of the spirit of Christ" is, for me, the key sentence in
the whole of the *Advices & Queries*: it is the single sentence which
captures our understanding of what we are called to be and to do.

This lecture explores the implications. If we are to carry out
this advice then we need to be able to determine what "the spirit
of Christ" requires of us. This is achieved by a process which
Friends call "discernment".

1.2 Discernment

The word "discern" is defined in the *Oxford English Dictionary*
to mean "to recognise as distinct", "to distinguish by the sight
or other senses". This does not convey all that Friends mean by
the word.

> In our meetings for worship we seek through the stillness
> to know God's will for ourselves and for the gathered
> group. Our meetings for church affairs, in which we
> conduct our business, are also meetings for worship based
> on silence, and they carry the same expectation that God's
> guidance can be discerned if we are truly listening together
> and to each other (*Quaker faith & practice* §3.02).[2]

The purpose of this lecture is to explore what is being
described here: the experience of discernment, what it is that we
are discerning, and the methods we use to achieve discernment.

The traditional God-language used in *Advices & Queries*
and elsewhere reflects an understanding of the nature of reality
which no longer seems tenable. It arose out of a religious world

view something like the following: God (a perfect, good, eternal, omnipotent, omniscient being) created the universe as a home for humanity; God allowed human beings free will, the power to make decisions; God rewards good actions and punishes bad actions; human life is a preparation for a greater life with God which comes, possibly only for some people, after death. I am uncomfortable with almost every aspect of this world view and I expect that most British Friends feel the same. However, I love the language and do not want to lose it. It reflects an *experience* of reality which is ours, too. We can use this language metaphorically, but to be true to our experience we have to do so from within a world view which we can uphold with integrity.

So before moving on to an exploration of discernment, of what we learn from our individual and corporate spiritual experiences, it is necessary for me to spend the first half of this lecture establishing a world view within which I can do so.

The approach I shall take is historical. It will focus on the development of scientific understanding in Europe, and the interplay between that and the development of Christian thought.

The structure of the lecture is as follows.

Chapter 2

§3.02 of *Quaker faith & practice*, quoted above, refers to "God's will". In order to begin to make sense of this I find that I need to clarify my understanding of God and God's rôle in the universe. What does it mean to think of God as the creator of the universe in the context of the present scientific understanding of the history of the universe? What is our understanding of "God's continuing creation"? I shall explore how our understanding of the physical world has developed, from a world in which actions by God (or gods) are required all the time to make things happen, to a world which appears to run itself with no help from God.

Chapter 3

Moving on to reflect on how God can then act in this world,
I encounter the problem of how we can reconcile God's actions
with the scientific laws governing the behaviour of the universe.
This brings me to the same difficulty in reconciling our own
actions with scientific law. So I have to consider to what extent
our actions are governed by scientific laws, and to what extent we
have free will. This raises the question of the place of humanity
in the universe. At one extreme there is the traditional view that
the universe was created to provide a home for humanity. At the
other extreme lies the view of some that human beings and indeed
all life is just an accidental by-product of the development of the
universe. Neither of these extreme views seems acceptable.

Chapter 4

This leads on to questions about the purpose of the universe and
the purpose of our own lives, and to questions about how we
reconcile suffering and evil with a loving God.

Chapter 5

I then need to consider our experience of the world around us
and of God. This challenges me to consider my own experience,
and in particular the various ways in which I believe that I have
experienced God. How do we understand, and how do we live in,
"God's presence"?

Chapter 6

This leads to a consideration of how we respond to this
experience, what we understand by "God's guidance" and how
this is an expression of "God's will". This requires consideration
of the principles underlying the Quaker process of corporate
discernment, of some recent experiences of discernment in
our yearly meeting, and of my own experiences of personal
discernment.

Chapter 7

Finally I come to the practice of Quaker discernment and my experience of the particular techniques that we have developed over the years. Friends' practice of discernment is grounded in our corporate worship and so this brings me back to the experience of meeting for worship and raises the question of the extent to which this practice depends on a common understanding of discipleship.

Undertaking this lecture is proving a humbling and sometimes unsettling experience. I shall reflect later about the experience of agreeing to do it as an example of personal discernment. But from the outset I feel it necessary to say that I have found it difficult to come to grips with what the passages from *Advices & Queries* and *Quaker faith & practice* quoted above require of us. So I hope that my words will be in right ordering. The psalmist says it better:

> May the words of my mouth, and the meditation of my heart, be acceptable in thy sight, O Lord, my strength, and my redeemer (Psalm 19:14, Authorised Version).[3]

CHAPTER 2
God's continuing creation

Before the hills were born and the world was:
from age to age Thou art God.

John Henry Newman, *The Dream of Gerontius*
(after Psalm 90:2). Set to music by Edward Elgar.

The passage on discernment quoted earlier from *Quaker faith & practice* §3.02 refers to our knowing God's will and discerning God's guidance. I need to explore what we understand by these phrases. But before doing this I need to consider the relationship between God and the world. *Advices & Queries* §42 refers to "God's continuing creation". What does this mean? To reflect on this we need some understanding of the nature of the universe.

As a child I spent my summers with my Auntie Lizzie and Uncle Jack at Woodside Bank, their house on the moors above Darwen in Lancashire. They had met through their mutual interest in Esperanto and through this had a very international outlook, travelling quite widely in Europe meeting local people through the medium of Esperanto. Uncle Jack worked as a labourer, but he was a well-educated working class man who had spent time at Ruskin College in Oxford in his early years. They were a remarkable couple to whom I owe a great deal.

One of Uncle Jack's many interests was astronomy. I still have the telescope through which he showed me the mountains of the moon, the moons of Jupiter, the phases of Venus and (with the help of a lot of imagination) the rings of Saturn. I imagine it was through his influence that I decided as a child that when I grew up I would be an astronomer. I don't think I ever am going to grow up – it is too late now. I recall discovering a whole shelf of books on astronomy in the Blackpool South Shore Library, my local library, but then to my dismay being told that I could not borrow these "adult" books with my junior ticket; I must have been nine or ten at the time. The problem was soon overcome.

For the purposes of this lecture, I want to go back to my childhood fascination with the cosmos to consider how we understand the universe, how we understand God's and our own place in it, and how we understand our relationship to God.

It has taken a long time for humanity's understanding of the physical universe to reach its present state. First came various pre-scientific approaches. Each culture had its own creation myth. These saw humanity and our relationship with a creator God (or gods) as having a central place in creation. Then, starting in the seventeenth century, there was the scientific revolution which led to the classical scientific view of a world which seemed mechanistic and deterministic, with no real place for God except possibly as the creator who set things going.

In the last 150 years this view has been significantly modified by various emerging ideas – evolution by natural selection, relativity theory and quantum mechanics – and by new observations of the distant universe and the very small; these have led to the modern scientific view. Modern physics has been enormously successful but these new ideas, particularly quantum mechanics, have also raised difficult questions about the true nature of reality. The discovery of evolution through natural selection raised questions about the place of humanity in the universe which I shall consider in the next chapter.

2.1 The pre-scientific world

It is normally considered that anatomically modern humans, *Homo sapiens sapiens*, first arose between 150,000 and 120,000 years ago, but only started to use their capabilities in a manner which we would recognise as fully human in a social and cultural sense between 60,000 and 20,000 years ago. It is difficult to know how and when human language developed (see §3.4). Records of written language go back only about 5,000 years (see Chris Gosden 2003, pp. 41–2 and p. 10).

Language permits the sharing of knowledge and stories so that a much richer corporate understanding of the world could develop. There is a collective knowledge and understanding which we can in principle all access, though each of us only possesses a very small part of it. The evolution of language must have taken place alongside the development of a conceptual understanding of the world, such as the ability to classify objects into categories, having a sense of cause, effect and purpose, being self-conscious, and being aware of the self-consciousness of others. All human societies must have attempted to understand the world in which they found themselves and have asked questions about the purpose of human lives. It is natural to ask about how the world was made, a questioning which then leads to the development of the creation stories which most cultures appear to have had.

Most of us are probably most familiar with the creation stories in Genesis. In these everything is created by a God who, pre-existing the world, must be outside it. Humanity has a central place in this creation.

> So God created man in his own image; in the image of God he created him; male and female he created them. God blessed them and said to them, "Be fruitful and increase, fill the earth and subdue it, rule over the fish in the sea, the birds of heaven, and every living thing that moves upon the earth." God also said, "I give you all plants that bear seed

everywhere on earth, and every tree bearing fruit which yields seed: they shall be yours for food" (Genesis 1:27–9, New English Bible).

So the world was seen as created to provide a home for humanity. God was seen not only as the creator but as actively engaged with the day-to-day running of his world. On this view, we rely on God to make sure that the sun rises each morning, that the seasons come on time, that the rains come when they are needed, that crops grow and ripen. God was seen (or, in some other cultures, gods were seen) as responsible for everything that happened – including bad things like earthquakes, floods or droughts.

In her 1995 Swarthmore Lecture, Anne Thomas explored the significance of various creation stories and, in particular, the stories in the book of Genesis. In these the creation of human beings was the climax of a series of events. The only aspect of the world not fully under God's control was the behaviour of human beings, because God gave us free will. Human beings were given the responsibility of naming all the other creatures, which implicitly gave us the authority of life and death over them – but also a responsibility for them:

> Genesis 1 presents a unique relationship between God and human beings, with God giving over power of governance and human beings becoming the agents to whom much is given and from whom much expected. There is both closeness and distance in the relationship between God and human beings. Closeness is the trust given to humankind; distance allows human beings to have the freedom of response to God (Anne Thomas 1995, p. 37).

God would respond to the behaviour of human communities or individual human beings and might reward or punish people for their behaviour. This was the accepted view in the seventeenth century and was accepted by early Friends. Consider the following story in George Fox's *Journal* about some events on 28 June 1657 at Frandley (where there is still a local meeting, now in my own area meeting of East Cheshire).

So…we returned back into England [from Wales] and… we came into Cheshire to William Gandy's [at Frandley]; and there we had a meeting of two or three thousand people; and the everlasting word of life was held forth and received that day. And a blessed meeting it was, for Friends were settled by the power of God upon Christ Jesus the rock and foundation.

And at this time there was a great drought; and after the General Meeting was ended there fell a mighty rain, and there was so much rain the next day that Friends said they believed we could not pass, the brooks and waters would be so risen; but I believed so far as they had come that day to the meetings so far they had rain. So the next day about the afternoon we came back into some parts of Wales again and there was all dust, and no rain had fallen thereabout, and it was a noted thing generally amongst people that when I came, still I brought rain, and it had been so for many years.

And when Oliver Protector gave forth a proclamation for a fast throughout the nation for rain when there was such a mighty drought; as far as Truth had spread in the north there was rain enough and pleasant showers, when up in the south in places they were almost spoiled for want of rain. And I was moved to give forth an answer to Oliver Protector's proclamation that if he did come to own God's truth he should have rain and that drought was a sign unto them of their barrenness of the water of life, as you may see in that book given forth in answer to his proclamation. And the like observation and expectation they have beyond the seas. When there is a drought they generally look for the Quakers' General Meetings, for then they

know they shall have rain; and as they receive the Truth
and become fruitful unto God, they receive from him their
fruitful seasons also (George Fox *Journal* 1975, pp. 292–93).

This indicates that George Fox saw God as rewarding the people
who accepted the Truth by supplying them with rain. Oliver
Cromwell also saw the best way of overcoming a drought as
being a national fast, fulfilling the same function as a rain dance
– although possibly not as much fun. The idea that natural
phenomena can be affected by ritualistic human actions would
have been generally accepted at that time.

2.2 The classical scientific world

Just four years after George Fox was at Frandley, Isaac Newton
entered Trinity College, Cambridge. In due course his work led to
a transformation of our view of the world.

The scientific method had its roots in the ideas of the ancient
Greeks. Aristotle approached the study of matter by basing it on
a small number of fundamental principles. However, he assumed
that these principles could be perceived as self-evident truths
which could be discovered by pure thought. For Aristotle, the
natural state of a body was to be at rest and so it would move
only if driven by a force or impulse. It was known that the earth
was a spherical object.[1] The earth was evidently stationary and
the centre of the universe. Material objects fell downwards from
a desire to reach the cosmic centre, unless they were heavenly
(light) objects in which case they moved upwards towards their
natural state in heaven.

The development of the Greek earth-centred system
culminated in a theory fully worked out by Claudius Ptolemaeus
(Ptolemy) around 150 CE in his book now known as the *Almagest*
("The Great Book").[2] Circles and spheres were seen as the
most perfect geometrical shapes and so, since the heavens were
considered perfect, they provided the means of describing the

position and motion of the heavens. The sun, the moon and the five known planets were each attached to a translucent sphere centred on the earth, each being carried around the earth in a circle by the rotation of its sphere.[3] The stars were positioned on an outer celestial sphere which also turned around the earth, beyond that lying the sphere of the "prime mover" (or God) who kept the whole mechanism turning.

In the thirteenth century Thomas Aquinas synthesised ancient Greek cosmology and physics with the church's doctrine: the earth was seen as the realm of fallen humanity, the heavens were the realm of God, and hell was at the centre of the earth.[4]

In fact, Aristarchus had suggested in the third century BCE that the planets, including the earth, revolved around the sun because his observations indicated that the sun is very much larger than the earth. Nearly two thousand years later, this idea was rediscovered by Nicholas Copernicus (1473–1543) who came to the conclusion that the ptolemaic system could be simplified if the sun were placed at the centre of the cosmos with the earth and planets moving in orbits around it. These orbits, though, were still based on circles and most of the complications of the ptolemaic system remained. Subsequently, Johannes Kepler (1571–1630) struggled to make the circular orbits of the Copernican theory fit in with the most recent more accurate observations of the position of Mars.[5] Suggesting that the planets were imperfect like the earth and so might have imperfect orbits, he proposed that the orbit of each planet is an ellipse[6] with the sun at one focus.[7]

More or less contemporary with Kepler was Galileo Galilei (1564–1642). In 1609 Galileo successfully marketed the newly invented telescope to the Venetian Senate as a weapon of war for detecting approaching ships (see Arthur Koestler 1964, p. 369). He then used the telescope to look at the night sky observing, amongst other things, mountains on the moon "just like the face of the earth itself", the four largest moons of Jupiter, and the phases of Venus, which he saw as being just like the moon's.

Galileo believed that these observations supported Copernicus' solar-centric system, for the moons of Jupiter showed that there were objects in the heavens which did not move in orbits centred on the earth, calling into question the whole basis of the ptolemaic system.

However, even more significant was Galileo's introduction of the experimental method to test Aristotle's assertions about motion. Possibly we all know the probably apocryphal story of his demonstration at the Leaning Tower of Pisa that bodies of different masses fall at the same rate under gravity, contradicting the accepted Aristotelian view that heavier objects fall more quickly. He certainly did perform experiments in order to demonstrate this. His key observation was that uniform motion is experimentally indistinguishable from rest, something which we can all experience on a smoothly moving train or aeroplane.[8] He set out his ideas in his great book *Dialogue on the Great World Systems,* published in 1632, not so long before George Fox was to propose an experimental approach to the study of religious ideas. The publication of this book led to the well-known dispute with the Church leading to Galileo's trial before the Inquisition in Rome in 1633.[9]

Isaac Newton (1642–1727), born in the year of Galileo's death, further developed Galileo's ideas to formulate his three laws of motion. Using these, he deduced from Kepler's laws that the motion of the planets was governed by a force of attraction towards the sun and that the strength of this force depended, in a strikingly simple way, on the distance between the planet and the sun. In addition, he was able to demonstrate that this force of gravity, which governed the motions of the moon and the planets, was the same as the force which pulled material objects down towards the centre of the earth. He suggested no mechanism for how this force operated; but he considered that every material object in the universe is attracted to every other material object by gravity.[10]

This work of Newton's has always struck me as one of the most spectacular mathematical achievements of all time. It laid the foundation for physics for the next 250 years even though the subject continued to develop, in particular by identifying electromagnetic forces. Even today, calculations can for most practical purposes be performed using the Newtonian theory. One consequence of this theory is that, if the position and velocity of every object in the universe were known at some moment in time, then this would determine the past and future of every object. This means that the theory implies that the universe is *deterministic*. I will shortly return to the difficulties that this creates.

2.3 The modern scientific world

If you want to make a man a useless fool, teach him logic and philosophy. Before that, he may have been fit for something, but after that he will be good for nothing but speaking nonsense.

Robert Barclay, quoted in
Patricia Williams (2007, p. 28)[11]

When I studied mathematics at school, the mechanics I learnt was essentially that introduced by Newton apart from some development in the mathematical techniques used. My study of Newtonian mechanics reached its climax in my first year at university when I learnt the spectacular theory of orbits, which governs planetary motion.

However, my general reading, building on those early "adult" books from the South Shore Library, had left me wanting to learn other things at university – my ambition was to learn about relativity theory and quantum mechanics.

Towards the end of the nineteenth century there was a widespread sense that all of physics was known. However, this was not to last, and early in the twentieth century these two new theories appeared. Relativity theory modifies Newtonian mechanics at very high velocities and leads to some strange apparent paradoxes regarding space and time as well as to the equivalence of matter and energy. Quantum mechanics modifies Newtonian mechanics at very small distances, producing some real difficulties in understanding the nature of the physical universe. Some of these are mentioned in §3.3.

Building on these theories and a wealth of observations, we now have a theory of the cosmos which is a refined version of that set out by Arthur Eddington in his 1929 Swarthmore Lecture *Science and the Unseen World*. His universe begins in a rather biblical way as a void sparsely populated by elementary particles which then condense into galaxies ("island universes"), which in turn condense into stars. One of Eddington's major contributions over the previous decade had been work on the structure of stars, and he had begun to explore the idea that the heat of stars might come from nuclear forces. At that time it was thought that only very few stars had planetary systems, these having been produced by a "rare accident".

Arthur Eddington was a major figure in physics at that time, playing a leading rôle in the development and acceptance of relativity theory. The year after his Swarthmore Lecture he lectured on the idea that the universe was expanding (A. Vibert Douglas 1956, p. 54). Albert Einstein had observed some years earlier that this was a consequence of his General Theory of Relativity but at the time modified the theory in order to obtain a static universe. However, later theoretical work suggested that a static universe was impossible. In 1929 Edwin Hubble observed that the universe was expanding, for when he studied the light from distant galaxies he found that the light was shifted towards the red end of the spectrum, indicating that those galaxies were moving away from us; the further away they were, the faster they were receding.[12] As a consequence, as we go back in time everything moves closer together.

In my student days there was still some controversy about the significance of this observation. One possibility was that the universe began from a highly compressed state (the "Big Bang") but some astronomers found the idea of a beginning of the universe unpalatable and suggested a process of continual creation of matter filling the gaps as the universe expanded (the "steady state universe"). The situation was finally resolved in 1965 when the cosmic background radiation predicted by the Big Bang theory was observed.

The generally accepted view today is that the universe began nearly 14,000 million years ago, exploding from a highly compressed state: the Big Bang. The beginning moment is a "singularity" at which the present known laws of physics do not apply. Since time and space were created at that moment, it makes no sense to talk about "before" that moment – any more than it does to refer to a point on the earth's surface south of the south pole (an analogy used by Stephen Hawking).

Since the moment of creation the universe has been expanding, possibly very rapidly indeed for a very short time at the beginning. There is now a fairly good theory of the development of the universe from an extremely short time after the Big Bang.[13] After a few minutes most of the matter in the universe consisted of positively charged nuclei of hydrogen and helium atoms with negatively charged electrons moving freely. After nearly 400,000 years most of the free electrons had become attached to the atomic nuclei forming stable atoms.[14]

These atoms eventually condensed to form galaxies and then the first generation of stars. In these stars the heavy elements formed, crucially including carbon and oxygen, and when the stars exploded as supernovae at the ends of their lives, these elements were scattered through the galaxy. The next generation of stars formed from matter including some of these heavy elements and our sun, at least, had planets some of which were formed from the heavy elements. The sun and our earth were formed about 4,500 million years ago.

The distances and times involved are hard to comprehend.

The distance from the earth to the sun is about 90 million miles which means that heat and light from the sun take a little more than eight minutes to get here – so the sun is just over eight "light minutes" away. The nearest star is over four light years away – about 270,000 times the distance of the sun. The Milky Way galaxy to which we belong is about 100,000 light years in diameter – that is, about 25,000 times the distance to the nearest star. Our galaxy is part of the "local group" of galaxies, a group with a diameter about 100 times the size of the Milky Way; and the Milky Way is due to collide with our nearest neighbour, the Andromeda galaxy, in about 3,000 million years. There are about 100,000 million stars in the Milky Way galaxy. The number of galaxies in the visible universe (the part of the universe that we can observe, which now has a radius of about 47,000 million light years), is similar.[15] And we know nothing about the universe beyond – which may be infinite and which may be completely different from the part of the universe we can observe, but which has no effect on us at all.

But what has happened to God? What place is there for God in this view of the universe? The pre-scientific world saw God as creator – the initiator of the universe, who was active in keeping it working from day to day. The classical scientific world began from the same basis, but the advent of the scientific method meant that the quest to understand how the world worked became separated from the quest to understand why it worked in that way, and from the attempt to understand its purpose.

The picture of the cosmos outlined above appears to leave no place for God, except possibly in the initial singularity of the Big Bang from which everything appeared.[16] So how can we now, if we accept the discoveries of modern science, understand God as presently active in the world?

The spirit of God at work

The modern view of the physical universe is of a vast cosmos, extremely cold and dark apart from widely separated galaxies which are flying apart from each other. Even within the galaxies the stars, mainly extremely hot, are great distances apart and, in the main, evolve extremely slowly. The whole choreography of the cosmic dance is determined by the laws of physics. If we are fortunate enough to find somewhere where light pollution is low, then at night we can gaze in wonder at the view of the cosmos from our planet, the earth, some 14,000 million years after it all began. Our view is informed by the observations of astronomers using modern equipment descended from the little telescope which Galileo first turned onto the heavens. Photographs taken by the Hubble space telescope reveal some amazing sights.

Reflecting on this vision of the universe can be an overwhelming experience. Even if we see this cosmos as created by God, it appears to be developing according to fixed laws which we now partly understand, without any need for God's active involvement. At the end of the previous chapter I indicated something of the size of the cosmos both in space and time. The Copernican displacement of the earth from its position at the centre of the universe has been so successful that it now appears completely insignificant in this vast universe.

And yet, this universe is our home. The meaning and significance of the universe may be completely beyond our comprehension. But we can wonder about our place in it and what it all means. We can always wonder. And, in a strange way, contemplating the cosmos brings us back to the intensely personal experience of the Presence in the Midst encountered in meeting for worship, for that is where we find meaning.

> And, behold, the Lord passed by, and a great and strong wind rent the mountains, and brake in pieces the rocks before the Lord; but the Lord was not in the wind: and after the wind an earthquake; but the Lord was not in the earthquake: and after the earthquake a fire; but the Lord was not in the fire: and after the fire a still small voice. ... And, behold, there came a voice unto him, and said, What doest thou here, Elijah? (1 Kings 19:11–13, Authorised Version)

This passage suggests that we will not find God in all the wonderful majesty of the cosmos, but closer to hand. Arthur S. Eddington quoted it too in his 1929 Lecture (p. 17–18).

3.1 God's action

The central place of God as creator in the pre-scientific world persisted to the time of Newton. Aristotle saw the planets as being moved by a "prime mover". Kepler considered that they were moved by angels.

Newton saw the universe as the work of God and believed that we could understand God by examining his work and his word:

> This most beautiful system of the sun, planets, and comets, could only proceed from the counsel and dominion of an intelligent and powerful Being. And if the fixed stars are the centres of other like systems, these, being formed by the like wise counsel, must all be subject to the dominion

of One; especially since the light of the fixed stars is of the
same nature as the light of the sun, and from every system
light passes into all other systems; and lest the systems
of the fixed stars should by their gravity, fall on each
other mutually, he hath placed these systems at immense
distances one from another (Isaac Newton 1995, p. 440).[1]

In bodies, we see only their outward figures and colours,
we hear only the sounds, we touch only their outward
surfaces, we smell only the smells, and taste the savours;
but their inward substances are not to be known either by
our senses, or by any reflex acts of our minds: much less,
then, have we any idea of the substance of God. We know
him only by his most wise and excellent contrivances of
things, and final causes; we admire him for his perfections;
but we reverence and adore him on account of his
dominion; for we adore him as his servants; and a god
without dominion, providence, and final causes, is nothing
else but Fate and Nature (p. 442).

Although Newton had some heretical religious views for his
time, he clearly saw God as an omniscient and omnipotent being.[2]
We now think of the classical scientific model of the universe
described by Newton as a clockwork universe. This was not
Newton's view. He saw the laws of physics as created by God, but
also saw God as actively engaged in ensuring that the laws were
followed. "Nothing is done without God's continual government
and inspection." Furthermore, Newton considered that God
would have to intervene from time to time, for example to ensure
that the solar system remained stable.

In the nineteenth century, Pierre de Laplace (1749–1827)
was able to demonstrate that the solar system could remain
stable, oscillating between fixed limits, so the universe could be
governed by Newtonian mechanics without the need for divine
intervention. This period also saw the beginnings of work on

how the solar system could have been formed naturally. Thus developed the view that the universe is deterministic for, as I have already mentioned, it is a mathematical consequence of Newton's theory of dynamics that the positions and velocities of all particles in the universe at any one moment determine the state of the universe at any time before or afterwards.

This leaves no way in which God could act in the world other than by overruling natural law. Even though our view of the laws of physics has changed considerably since the time of Laplace this dilemma remains, representing a major interest for writers on science and religion today. Of course, many religious people have no difficulty with the idea that God is not bound by the natural laws of the universe since "God is omnipotent". However, my starting point is that there is order in the universe and that both science and religion are seeking to understand this order, a pattern of behaviour for everything including God. If God is able to act, then this pattern, the natural law, must somehow leave room for such action.

So far I have only considered the physical universe with no reference to living things and in particular to humanity. An even greater dilemma arises for us from the concept of the deterministic universe, suggesting as it does that *our* actions too are determined. All our experience leads us to believe that this is not the case, that we do have an element of free will.

Our ability to choose how we act is the basis of both morality, which would have no meaning without choice, and the religious quest. So, in seeking to understand how God might be active in the world, I am led to consider how we human beings can act. What is the extent of our own free will? If a deterministic universe leaves no way for God to act freely, then surely it leaves no such way for us, either.

So before pursuing further the question of how God acts in the world, let us think about our own actions. To do this we have to try to understand a little of how we come to be here and to explore the place of humanity in creation.

3.2 The origin of life

Given the scale of the universe, we appear very insignificant. On the pre-scientific world model we lived in a world which had been fashioned as a home for us at the centre of creation. This was the background to orthodox Christian doctrine. In the modern cosmic order, human beings appear to be almost incidental. Stephen Hawking is quoted by Paul Davies as saying that "the human race is just a chemical scum on a moderate-sized planet" (Paul Davies 2006, p. 251), a complete contrast to the pre-scientific world view and indeed to the view of most people of faith. Is it really possible that human beings, and indeed life itself, are accidental by-products of the evolution of the universe? It is clear that most of the universe seems to be extremely hostile to life. It may well be that in the whole of our solar system the only place where life can exist without artificial support is on or near the surface of the earth.

When the earth was formed about 4,500 million years ago it was a hot body whose first atmosphere and oceans were probably formed of methane, ammonia, water and carbon dioxide. There were violent electrical storms and a great deal of volcanic activity, an environment apparently hostile to life: human beings certainly could not have survived. We do not yet understand how, over the course of the next 1,500 million years, self-replicating molecules appeared but, once they did, more complex entities evolved by a process of random mutation and natural selection; this led to plants and animals and eventually to human beings.

It is just 150 years since Charles Darwin published his book *On the origin of species by means of natural selection, or the preservation of favoured races in the struggle for life*, setting out his theory of natural selection. The way in which evolution takes place and in which creatures of the complexity of human beings can develop has been beautifully explained by Richard Dawkins.[3] Strikingly, although it appears to have taken an enormously long time for self-replicating molecules to appear, once life did appear it soon spread over most of the planet, apart from a few particularly hostile places, and was able to survive several major catastrophes.

I learnt about evolution as a child from my mother, who used to tell me about her evening classes on genetics, and so I have always taken the theory for granted without thinking about the details. My work on this lecture has helped me to appreciate how remarkable it is. We may have difficulty understanding how self-replicating molecules can appear spontaneously and then how natural selection can combine with random mutations to produce extremely complex features in the structure and behaviour of living things (such as the eye, nest-building by birds, or the social structure of a bee colony); this difficulty is not surprising given the unimaginably big timescales involved. Richard Dawkins (2006, chapter 6) thoroughly discusses some of the probability issues of the initial appearance of life on earth. Through the last 3,000 million years species have appeared, disappearing again with the development of other species better adapted to the shifting environment of the time. The environment is always changing as a result of natural physical forces, such as the cooling of the earth, or as a consequence of the activity of living things.

There have been a number of catastrophic events through the history of our planet, which have led to mass extinctions of species and consequently to a dramatic acceleration in evolution. The most recent and best known led to the extinction of the dinosaurs. This is known as the Cretaceous-Tertiary extinction event and occurred about 65 million years ago. It now seems likely that this event was caused by an asteroid colliding with earth, although other causes have been considered (see Michael Allaby and James Lovelock 1983). The extinction allowed mammals and birds to become the dominant land vertebrates and so opened the way for the eventual evolution of human beings. The largest known extinction event is the Permian- Triassic extinction event which occurred about 251 million years ago. This, known as "the great dying", wiped out an estimated 96 per cent of all marine species and an estimated 70 per cent of land species, including plants, insects and vertebrate animals; it created the opportunity for the dinosaurs to become, in due course, the dominant land vertebrates. Thus such extinction events have been crucial for the progress of evolution.[4]

Living creatures themselves affect their own environment. For example, the oxygen-rich atmosphere essential for our survival has been created by the impact of a whole variety of species. Human beings in their turn have modified the environment, particularly through the introduction of agriculture, which was a crucial step in our development. However, since the industrial revolution, our impact on the environment has been even more dramatic, and the likely consequences of this are now alarming. What is striking is the resilience of the planet and of life. As a result of our actions the planet might become unsuitable for human life. However, our actions are unlikely to make it unsuitable for all life. If human beings become extinct then other species will move in to take our place. Life appears to be remarkably persistent.

It is difficult to envisage a world different from how it is. When someone we love dies we struggle to adjust to a world without them – but we do not have to adjust to a world in which they have never been, and we can still take pleasure in our memories of them. I suppose that we are now familiar with the idea that our individual existence with its own unique genetic make-up, arising from the union of a particular sperm with a particular ovum, is just an accident – in fact the result of an enormous chain of accidents right back to when life first appeared on earth. I can envisage a universe in which I do not exist. If we reflect on Darwinian evolution then we might also manage to envisage, on the same grounds, a universe in which the species of Homo sapiens with its particular genetic make-up does not exist. We might even contemplate that, if it took 1,500 million years for life to appear on the earth, then maybe the earth could have existed for 4,500 million years without it yet having appeared. However, to go further and contemplate a universe without life at all, in particular without self-conscious life, seems bleak indeed. It would appear to remove all meaning from the universe. If the universe has any meaning and purpose, that must surely be realised through self-conscious living creatures. But then a living self-conscious creature would say that, wouldn't he?

3.3 Why is there life in the universe?
A number of scientists have worked on the question of why there is life in the universe. It appears that it is only possible because the laws of the universe and a number of constants of nature take the precise values that they do. For example, there are the ratios between the strength of different forces such as gravity and electromagnetism or between the masses of different particles. If these constants were different, then it seems that galaxies and stars could not have formed and the chemistry of the universe would have been completely different. It is usually assumed that for life to exist then the laws of physics must lead to the formation of material structures such as galaxies and stars, to the creation of an element such as carbon whose atoms are able to combine with other atoms to form the complex molecules required for biology, and to the appearance of places where the vital components of life can come together and have time to evolve. It is conceivable of course that in a radically different universe life could arise that is quite different to the life that we know. Life, though, surely requires highly complex structures and it is hard to see how these could emerge in any other way. It seems that the physical "laws" necessary for these things to happen are very restrictive. Paul Davies calls this "the Goldilocks factor" of the universe.

> Like the porridge in the tale of Goldilocks and the three bears, the universe appears to be "just right" for life, in many intriguing ways. No scientific explanation for the

universe can be deemed complete unless it accounts for this appearance of judicious design (Paul Davies 2006, p. 3).[5]

There is another element of the fine-tuning which relates to the second law of thermodynamics. This can be summarised as follows:

Heat won't pass from a cooler to a hotter,
You can try it if you like but you'd far better notter,
'Cos the cold in the cooler will get hotter as a ruler,
'Cos the hotter body's heat will pass to the cooler,
Oh you can't pass heat, cooler to a hotter,
Try it if you like but you'll only look a fooler
'Cos the cold in the cooler will get hotter as a ruler
And that's a physical Law![6]

Michael Flanders and Donald Swann,
"First and second law" (1963)

The significance of the second law is that it gives a direction to time. The laws of physics given by Newton, and Einstein for that matter, are time-symmetrical and do not distinguish between moving forwards and backwards in time. However, our everyday experience is that there is a tremendous difference. If we watch a film backwards then there is clearly something wrong. It is not just that people look strange walking backwards, for presumably we could learn to do this, but that we see chaos moving into order: a spilt drink remarkably flows back into the glass, a broken plate remarkably comes back together into a whole plate. When I was a child I broke with a yo-yo a plate hanging on the wall which had been painted by my Auntie Amanda. My mother spent hours fitting the pieces back together but it was never the same; it now hangs in our hall and serves as a reminder of the foolishness of playing with a yo-yo indoors. (I don't do that any more, though I do other foolish things.) How often would we love to reverse time in order to rectify the fact that "we have left undone those things which we ought to have done; and we have done those things which we ought not to have done" (from the General Confession in the Book of Common Prayer). However, time has a clear direction and there is no going back.

The direction of time is indicated by an increase in what is called entropy, which can be thought of as a measure of disorder. An increase in order leads to a reduction in entropy whereas an increase in disorder leads to an increase in entropy.[7] The second law of thermodynamics states that the entropy of a closed system never decreases or, equivalently, that order never increases of its own accord. In fact, according to this law, any system moves towards a condition of maximum entropy (disorder), sometimes called thermal equilibrium. For example, if you take a loaf of bread out of the oven and stand it on the kitchen table then the bread will cool to the same temperature as the kitchen, and the temperature of the kitchen will rise a little if it is better insulated than ours, "'Cos the hotter body's heat will pass to the cooler". In order for change to take place you need to start from a state of less than maximum entropy, in other words from a state with some element of order. A thermally sealed tank of water at a uniform temperature will continue unchanging in that state for ever.

After the Big Bang, the matter and energy in the universe was distributed with spectacular uniformity so that the total entropy of the universe was extremely low; this is in fact one of the most striking aspects of the fine-tuning of the early universe.[8] Since then the entropy of the universe has been steadily increasing: the formation of the galaxies and stars, the nuclear reactions in the stars, the explosions of the supernovae, the formation of the earth, the cooling of the earth and the resulting earthquakes and eruptions: these are all evidence of increasing entropy.

The reader may now be puzzled as to how we, and indeed all living things, fit into this. For we are creatures of amazingly ordered complexity. We only function because of the wonderfully subtle way our components fit together. How have we appeared in this universe which is becoming ever more disordered? The situation is that, although the overall entropy of a system increases when a system is, like the universe, far from equilibrium, in part of the system entropy can decrease – in other words, order can increase in that part.

This occurs when heat passes from a hot object to a cool object, like from my loaf of bread to our kitchen. The entropy of the hot loaf decreases as it cools and the entropy of the cool kitchen increases as it warms up. However, the increase in the entropy of the cool object is greater than the decrease in the entropy of the hot object so that there is an overall increase in accordance with the second law.[9] I was struck by Roger Penrose's account of the importance of the sun for our survival: its true significance is not as a source of heat and light but as our primary source of low entropy. The earth radiates more or less the same amount of energy as it receives from the sun but the radiated energy has much higher entropy, because it is cooler than the sun. Plants make use of the low-entropy energy in photosynthesis, thus reducing their entropy. We then eat the plants, or eat the animals which have eaten the plants, and breathe the oxygen which the plants release; this reduces our entropy (Roger Penrose 2004, p. 705).

One possible answer to the question of why the universe is fine-tuned for life is that, because self-conscious living beings are here to ask the question, the universe had to have been fine-tuned in this way, otherwise self-conscious living beings would not have existed. This is sometimes called the "anthropic principle" and doesn't really help.[10] It is inevitable that we find ourselves living in a universe in which is possible for self-conscious beings to exist, but this does not explain why such a universe exists.

There are those who see the fine-tuning of the universe as evidence that it was designed for life by a creator God (see for example John Lennox 2007, chapter 4). This is a version of intelligent design theory which is rather different from that of the religious fundamentalists who would like intelligent design taught alongside, or in place of, evolution by Darwinian natural selection. In the extreme form of fundamentalist intelligent design, biblical myths are treated as history and it has even been calculated that the creation took place on 23 October 4004 BCE, at 9 am.[11] However, the notion that God fine-tuned the laws of universe is a view which is consistent with Newton's view of God expressed in the first quote in §3.1.

I have real difficulty thinking of God as a creator in this way. Let us review how the ideas have developed. From a starting point which attributed the creation and functioning of the universe to God, scientific investigations first replaced God's involvement in the running of the universe with scientific laws, but then discovered that these laws are so finely tuned that it seems that they must have been designed by a Creator – so we are back where we started.

The God which I experience in the gathered meeting for worship is part of the universe, an aspect of how the universe is, an essential and natural part of the universe. I cannot relate to the notion of a God who is outside the universe acting upon it. This seems to be like asking a character in a play or novel to understand the concept of the author. There are of course plays and novels in which the characters address the author but, for me, these only succeed in confirming the absurdity of the idea.

I will come back to the idea of God's purposes and our experience of them in the next chapter. First, I shall consider the related issue of the existence of a self-conscious form of life, with the ability to make decisions.

In an attempt to understand the apparent fine-tuning of the universe, some scientists have put forward the idea of multiple universes in which all possible universes do exist and we (of course) find ourselves in one which is fine-tuned for life.[12] This seems unsatisfying partly because it leads to an enormous number of bleak lifeless universes. The idea that the earth is the only planet on which self-conscious life has evolved is almost as bleak, when we contemplate the vastness of the universe. The resilience of life on earth appears to indicate a fecundity which surely has found expression in other places. However, various researchers have calculated the probability of self-conscious life evolving, leading some to conclude that "it is unlikely to have occurred on any other planet in the entire visible universe" (John Barrow and Frank Tipler 1986, p. 133).[13]

Other scientists seek some understanding of the interconnections between the elements of the fine-tuning in the hope of discovering that in order for the laws of physics to be consistent, there is only one way that the universe could be. If this were the outcome it would mean that the universe is fine-tuned as it is because no other way was possible. This would be extremely satisfying to a mathematician.

Connected to this approach is the suggestion that the presence of self-conscious life (or observers) is necessary for the functioning of the universe.[14] Supporting arguments arise from the nature of quantum mechanics, in which conscious observers appear to have a particular rôle. Quantum mechanics is a highly successful but very mysterious theory which appears to deny ordinary physical reality. Much present-day technology is based upon it. Richard Feynman, one of the giants of the subject, wrote in 1967, "I think I can safely say that nobody understands quantum mechanics." This is not the place to go into any detail, even if I were competent to do so. However, I need to say something.

In quantum mechanics, an electron – to take this as an example – is not considered to be a particle or a wave but is represented by something called a wave function, which is an abstract mathematical concept. The way this wave function changes in time is completely deterministic, governed by an equation called Shrödinger's equation. According to the Copenhagen interpretation of quantum mechanics put forward by Niels Bohr and Werner Heisenberg in the late 1920s and considered to be the orthodox interpretation of quantum mechanics, part of the information in the wave function is the probability of finding the electron at any given point when an observation is made.[15] Usually there is a region of space where the electron is most likely to be. When the observation is made, the electron is found to be at some particular spot. As a result of this observation the wave function "collapses" into a special wave function, which corresponds to the electron being in the place where it was found at the moment of the observation.

However, another aspect of the Copenhagen interpretation is the Heisenberg uncertainty principle. According to this, the more accurately you determine the position of the electron the less you can know about its velocity: it is impossible, not only in practice but in principle, to know both the position and velocity with complete precision. If you know where it is, you don't know where it is going! One way of thinking of this is that the act of observing the position of an electron disturbs its velocity. There does not appear to be complete agreement about what constitutes an "observer", but it does appear to involve consciousness.

The origins of quantum mechanics lie in the study of the very small, at the level of atoms or elementary particles. However, according to the theory, everything can be represented by a wave function, but for larger objects the uncertainty about the position and the velocity is usually very small in relation to the size of the object. Nevertheless, according to the Copenhagen interpretation, the properties of all objects are "created" by the observation of them.

I will return to the question of how we observe the universe around us (§5.1). For the moment my purpose is to conclude that, although we may have abandoned the idea that the universe was created by God as a home for humanity, and although humanity and indeed the whole earth are incredibly small on a cosmic scale, it seems clear that there is a close relationship between precise details of the laws of nature and the existence of self-conscious life. Our place in the universe is still a mystery.

3.4 Human consciousness

Historically, human beings have been seen as somehow different in nature from other living things. So, for example, René Descartes (1596–1650) saw animals as biological machines made by God but with no reason or free will as in his Discourse on the method (1985 p. 139). He argued that human beings are different because we can communicate with each other, usually using words, and because we can reason and have intelligence. Human beings are also biological machines. In addition, though, they have an immortal rational soul which though specially created and of a completely different substance from the body, has freedom of action and the ability to interact with and control the body. Descartes even identified the pineal gland in the brain as the place where this interaction takes place, for example in The Passions of the Soul (1985 p. 340). The idea that the "soul" or "mind" or "consciousness" is distinct from the "brain" is known as dualism. There are real problems in understanding how the mind can interact with and indeed direct the brain.[16] Nevertheless, this idea has persisted and is very powerful in religious thought.

In Arthur Eddington's Swarthmore Lecture, he appeared to accept dualism and was dismissive of the suggestion that "the dance of atoms in the brain really constitutes the thought" (Arthur S. Eddington 1929, p. 19). The neurologist John Eccles in his Eddington Memorial Lecture (which I heard as a student in Cambridge) came to the same conclusion (John Eccles 1965, p. 42). However, I find the dualist point of view unsatisfactory, partly because of the difficulty in seeing how the mind and the brain can interact if they are separate entities and partly because of difficulty in understanding how such a mind could emerge by evolution. I prefer to take the materialist view that the mind is somehow generated by the activity of the human brain. Daniel Dennett is a leading exponent of this point of view.

The human brain is an enormously complex system. For example the number of neurons in a human brain is of the same order as the number of stars in the Milky Way galaxy (about 100,000 million), whereas a honey bee has about one million and a primitive worm about 300. Each neuron in a human brain has about 2000 synapses (connections with other neurons), so there are about 100 million million of these in each human brain.[17] It seems conceivable that consciousness might arise from all this complexity. Indeed, Douglas Hofstadter (2007) has argued that the sense of selfhood and so of consciousness is an inevitable consequence of the complex way our brains structure our perceptions of the world around us.

This is an area where there is quite a bit of controversy. I accept John Searle's view that "consciousness is an ordinary biological phenomenon comparable with growth, digestion, or the secretion of bile. ... The brain is an organ like any other; it is an organic machine. Consciousness is caused by lower-level neuronal processes in the brain and is itself a feature of the brain" (John R. Searle 1997, pp. 6 and 17).[18] However, it seems that our normal model of a single "stream of consciousness" progressing linearly through time is a great simplification, even though it is how it feels to us most of the time. It seems clear that our brains operate as parallel processors with an immensely complex web of interconnected strands of "thought" going on, most of it in our unconscious. So while I am writing this text and concentrating on the words, I am also aware of the sun in the garden, the meal I started to prepare a few minutes ago, a mathematical problem I have been working on, and no doubt many other things; at any moment any one of them may pop up and demand attention.

Daniel Dennett considers how consciousness might have evolved (1993, chapter 7). He discusses how evolution might have led first to the "hard-wiring" of the brain which enables creatures to perform remarkably complicated acts such as nest-building or web-spinning. Then plasticity evolved in the brain, allowing for greater learning from experience. Many creatures are born and are immediately able to live independent lives – they may not have any contact with their parents. However, the great dependence of human babies on adults is crucial for their social development: they need to live in close proximity to their parents (or other adults) for several years. So the lack of hard-wiring in the human brain is immensely beneficial, even though it leads to vulnerability in the short term. Daniel Dennett suggests that the human brain, "an enormously complex brain of unrivalled plasticity", had already evolved about 150,000 years ago.

A key feature in the evolution of humans is the development of language, alongside the development of social relationships and a rich culture.

Written language appears only to have been in existence for five or six thousand years but the origin of spoken language is not known. Robins Burling suggests that the evolution of the capacity for language may have taken several million years (2005, pp. 150–51). He links the expansion of the brain, which began with *Homo erectus* about two million years ago, to the development of language and social skills. In contrast, Daniel Dennett (1993, pp. 189–90) seems clear that language developed after the human brain had evolved and that the remarkable expansion of human mental powers has all happened in the last 10,000 years. Chris Gosden suggests (2003, p. 118) that the great upsurge in human symbolism – rock art, carved figures and the decoration of objects – about 40,000 years ago is significant. The most common view appears to be that language has existed for about 50,000 years and it is generally accepted that the capacity for language is hard-wired into human brains.

A degree of consciousness is present in many creatures. There is no sharp line between creatures with consciousness and creatures without it. Human beings appear to differ primarily in our degree of consciousness and in particular in our self-consciousness or self-awareness. In addition, the use of language appears to have had a dramatic effect on the way that our minds work as well as enabling immensely rich social development.

As well as individual consciousness, group intelligence and consciousness are also significant when the interconnections between the members of the group lead to behaviour and knowledge which can only be described in terms of the whole group. We are aware of this when we see a flock of birds wheeling in the sky, moving as one organism, or in the behaviour of a hive of bees or of a nest of ants. Humans exhibit crowd behaviour too, particularly in situations when large numbers come physically together, such as sporting events, when the individual behaviour is modified by its participation in the group. However, our emphasis on individuality means that we normally have to work quite hard to develop group behaviour, say in rehearsing a musical or theatrical performance or training to play as a team. Meeting for worship is a group activity during which we find that our individual awareness is modified by the group behaviour. Effective participation benefits from practice.

3.5 How human beings act in the world

So what about free will? It is possible to imagine consciousness and self-consciousness without free will, and indeed Daniel Dennett and Douglas Hofstadter consider that free will is an illusion or an irrelevance. However, as I have observed above, the reality of free will is crucial for us, since it is necessary if decision-making is to be real and so if morality is to have any meaning. The exploration of free will by philosophers appears to be even more fraught than the exploration of consciousness. In working on this lecture I found it difficult to get beyond this point because of the difficulties I encountered in understanding the issues. The most helpful book I have found is *A contemporary introduction to free will* (2005) by Robert Kane.

The basic problem is this. If the universe is deterministic, then each event is determined by previous events. So each event is inevitable. This means that if human consciousness is determined by our brain activity even our thoughts are determined and so any choices we make are determined, though it might feel as we have made free choices. On the other hand, even if the universe is not fully deterministic there is still a problem, for if there is some element of chance, such as appears in the Copenhagen interpretation of quantum mechanics, then to the extent that these chance events affect our consciousness and our choices, these choices are determined by chance.

It seems difficult to reconcile this with our experience that we *do* make real choices all the time. However, it is surprising to see what philosophers can manage. Robert Kane explains that "an increasingly popular doctrine in modern philosophy" is "compatibilism": the view that there is no conflict between determinism and free will (2005, p. 12). This approach requires us to make a distinction between freedom of action and freedom of decision-making. Free will is identified with freedom of action, which means that there are no constraints preventing me from doing what I want to do. However, the choices we make are determined by past events, including our past brain states, and the decisions we make are the culmination of a sequence of past events, including our thoughts. Nevertheless, these are real choices for which we must take responsibility, even though determinism implies that there is only one possible future.

I suppose it is a matter of perspective. If we could see the whole picture then we would see that the future was determined, but as players in the action it is not possible to know this and we are caught up in what we experience as a genuine choice, just as a character in a novel with whom we identify as we enter the world of the novel may appear to have a genuine choice. This point of view seems similar to the view that free will is an illusion but I suspect that its proponents would not agree. They may consider that the our experience of free will includes the need to consider the consequences of our actions and the need to take responsibility for them.

There is a clearly an element of truth in the compatibilist

approach, for we are increasingly aware of how our decisions are affected by our genetic make-up and our upbringing, which help shape our unconscious thoughts. We can never be certain that we are in control. There is a strange relationship between time and consciousness so that, for example, our memory of the order in which events take place can be incorrect, and actions which we believe we willed may have taken place before we were conscious of making those choices. This means that the decision must have been made unconsciously and our belief that the decision was made consciously is an illusion (see Roger Penrose 1989, p. 568 onwards).

However, what determinism would not appear to permit is human creativity. It seems inconceivable to me that all the creations of the human mind and spirit are either inherent in the universe from its beginning or alternatively are the result of chance. The development of complex structures, life and self-conscious beings may well have been inevitable. Presumably, the exact form of these structures and these living beings is partly the result of chance. So although I might find beauty in the sight of the rings of Saturn, the shape of a mountain or the sound of a bird singing, their precise forms do not have any particular significance. We might marvel that these things have emerged from the Big Bang but we can probably accept that a combination of determinism and chance has produced them. They are like a piece of "found art" and our recognition of their beauty is a creative act. On the other hand, supreme works of creativity such as the Beethoven string quartets seem to carry a meaning which is something new. Beethoven is said to have agonised over each note, for the choice of note mattered. To go from the sublime to the ridiculous, even this Swarthmore Lecture is something new, and I make constant choices about what to include and which words to use. It is free will which allows for this sort of creativity.

At first sight it may seem that dualism might solve the problem: my mind (or soul, the real "me", seen as something apart from the body) acts as an agent controlling my body rather like a puppet, presumably exploiting some element of indeterminism in the physical world. I decide to raise my arm, then I do raise my arm, with my brain somehow playing the role of the string between my mind and my arm. However, the problem with this appears to be that the difficult issues about determinism and chance are simply pushed back to the behaviour of my mind: either the actions by my mind are determined by my previous mental states or there is an element of chance about what the mind does. It is no more clear how free will, the real "me", can reside in a separate mind than it is clear how it can reside in a mind determined by the brain. Nor is it clear what "mind" separated from "brain" can mean.

3.6 Explanations for free will

Scientists are beginning to look for possible avenues for free will, compatible with current scientific understanding.

I have already mentioned the probabilistic aspects of quantum mechanics: elementary particles are represented by a "wave function" which determines the probability of various outcomes when the particle is observed. This means that when an observation takes place the outcome is undetermined in advance and so appears to produce a random element into the development of the universe. Roger Penrose has suggested that there is some procedure which determines the outcome of an observation so that it is not in fact random (1989, p. 558 and pp. 577–78). His idea is that this would resolve some major difficulties in reconciling relativity theory and quantum mechanics. He suggests that "once [the procedure] has been actually found, it may *then* become possible to elucidate the phenomenon of consciousness in terms of it."

A second approach to the way in which free will might exist is explored by John Polkinghorne, whose lectures on quantum mechanics I attended as a student. Since those days, he has become an Anglican clergyman and a prolific writer on science and religion from a traditional theological standpoint. He explores the question of how human beings and God can be free to act, but rejects the suggestion that the uncertainty in quantum mechanics might provide a mechanism for freedom of action (see for example John C. Polkinghorne 2005, p. 34). He suggests that "the aggregation of individually chance events is likely to compose itself into a highly predictable pattern at a higher level". This does seem to be borne out by the fact that larger objects normally do behave in a deterministic way.

John Polkinghorne's alternative is to consider "the subtlety of behaviour enjoyed by complex dynamical systems". It is important to understand that there is a real difference between behaviour being determined and behaviour being predictable. When we toss a coin the outcome is presumably *determined* by the force and angle of the flick we give the coin, the height we let it fall and possibly the movement of the air around the coin – but it is not predictable. In fact, this lack of predictability is very common. Historically, physics has concentrated on simple predictable systems such as a planet orbiting a star (a two-body problem) or a swinging pendulum. These are predictable because a small change in the state of the system produces a small change in the behaviour. However, most systems are not like this. If you consider two planets orbiting a star (a three-body problem) or a double pendulum, then the behaviour can become completely unpredictable because a very small change in the state of the system can produce a dramatic change in behaviour. Since we can only measure the state of the system approximately we cannot predict future behaviour even approximately. This is sometimes called the "butterfly effect" – the idea that a butterfly stirring the air on one side of the planet might affect the weather on the other side of the planet some time later because the weather is not a simple system: a small change in the state of the system (caused by the beating of the butterfly's wings) might subsequently lead to large changes in the future development of the system.

This example may be misleading since we all know that the weather is unpredictable because the earth's atmosphere is such a complex system. In fact very simple mathematical systems can give rise to behaviour which is essentially unpredictable or "chaotic". This means that, although a system might in principle be deterministic, it may not be possible to predict the future of the system even approximately. There are two problems: one is that it is not possible to measure the state of a system at a given moment with complete accuracy, the other is that any system is in principle affected by everything else in the observable universe.[19] John Polkinghorne suggests that "if you are realist and believe... that what we know... and what is the case... are closely linked to each other, it is natural to interpret this state of affairs as reflecting an intrinsic openness in the behaviour of these systems" (2005, p. 35). He sees this openness as providing the flexibility necessary for "God's purposive action in the world".

This openness does not mean that there is complete disorder. Mathematicians have discovered over the last 40 years or so that chaotic systems can display patterns of behaviour which can be studied. These patterns can only be seen if you examine not just one but the full range of possibilities for the behaviour of the system. James Gleick gives a readable account of the mathematics involved in this and a range of applications in *Chaos: making a new science* (1987).

There is another way of looking at this which has been investigated by the Quaker scientist George Ellis.[20] The key idea here is that of hierarchies of complexity.

Let me try to indicate what this is about. We sometimes imagine that to understand something properly we must always look at its component parts. This is called reductionism. However, this often does not appear to work, for when we look at the component parts, meaning disappears. For example, if you apply reductionism to a piece of music, the music disappears. A given note may be beautiful but that is only one part of the music. The music really lies in the relationship between the notes. In fact there is a whole hierarchy of structure. The individual notes form chords, tunes and rhythmical patterns and the structure of the music comes from relationships between these. And in the end the "meaning" of the music (whatever that might mean) lies in the context of a whole range of shared musical experience between the composer and the hearer.

Maybe this idea is clearer when we think about language since the concept of meaning is fundamental there. Where does the meaning in a passage of prose lie? Each word has meaning, but often there is ambiguity, and it is necessary to consider the sentence as a whole to tease out what is appropriate. In fact the sentence itself may require a paragraph to make sense of it – and that in turn may depend on the document in its entirety and even, as with the music, a whole range of shared experience between writer and reader.

Similarly, we can study the world around us at different levels (see George Ellis 2008, chapter 3, for a discussion of this). For example, when considering human behaviour, the lowest level may be taken to be particle physics which studies the particles making up atoms; examples of higher levels are chemistry (the study of molecules), biology (cells and living organisms), psychology (the mind) and sociology (communities). The reductionist viewpoint is that behaviour at each level is caused by behaviour at the level below so in the end everything is caused by the lowest level; "bottom-up causation is all there is". George Ellis argues that there is also "top-down action in this hierarchy of structure: the top levels influence what happens at the lower levels. They do so *inter alia* by setting the context in which the lower level actions function, thereby organising the way lower level functions integrate together to give higher level functions." He then gives examples of human actions to illustrate this: the way our brains are "able to coordinate the action of many millions of electrons and protons in such a way that it makes my arm move as I desire." Properties of a system which cannot be reduced to lower levels are called "emergent".

I do not profess to understand this fully. However, it provides a useful approach. It does not remove the problem of determining the source of freedom in the conscious mind since "there must be a looseness in the causal order – slippage at the bottom so to speak – so that the event is not over-determined causally" (Nancey Murphy and George Ellis 1996, p. 36). Finding this looseness in the causal order in the indeterminacies of quantum mechanics may be unsatisfactory, as I have already indicated; nevertheless, as has been pointed out by Keith Ward (2006, p. 94), quantum indeterminacy does demonstrate that there is no scientific barrier to indeterminism at the everyday level. "Once the stern grip of determinism has been loosened at the quantum level, we might be more open to the possibility of a macroscopic universe that is not bound by determinism."

Robert Kane refers to something called the "Real or Deep Self which one *identifies* or to which one is *wholeheartedly* committed", which some philosophers consider "cannot ... be wholly determined by something outside or beyond your own self. You yourself must be in part responsible for being the kind of person you are" (Robert Kane 2005, pp. 172–73). This seems compatible with George Ellis' approach but leaves the problem of finding a mechanism for free will.

This is a very difficult area. Superficially it seems simple. I recognise that the decisions I make are strongly influenced and sometimes even determined by my nature, my upbringing and often by influences I am not aware of. However, I remain convinced that I have some choices, in particular moral and creative ones, and that in the end I am responsible for these choices. We might say that an element of free will is an emergent property of our minds. However, once we start to seek a mechanism for this emergent property we seem to have real difficulty. Nevertheless, for the remainder of this lecture I shall assume that such choices are real.

I count not myself to have apprehended.

The closing words of Michael Tippett's
The vision of Saint Augustine.

This is a highly complex piece of music but, at the close, the chorus simply speaks these words in unison.

CHAPTER 4

God's purposes

Modern scientific ideas do not yet seem able to address questions of meaning and purpose although when we consider the place of life in the universe, such questions are highlighted. To understand consciousness and free will it will be necessary to find ways of exploring the higher levels of complexity identified by George Ellis. If we cannot understand how we can act, then there seems little chance of understanding God's actions.

There is an interesting extension of George Ellis' approach in the writings of Ken Wilber which I came across via Patricia Williams' book on Quaker theology, *Quakerism: a theology for our time* (2007). Ken Wilber writes of "the great nest of being" which is a hierarchy with physics (matter) at the bottom; above it come life (biology), then mind (psychology), soul (theology) and finally spirit (mysticism). Each higher level adds some features not found on the lower levels. Ken Wilber sees modernity as the differentiation of three "cultural values spheres": art (which seeks beauty and uses "I" language), morals (which seeks good and uses "we" language) and science (which seeks truth and uses "it" language). He sees this differentiation, which emerged in European culture starting in the seventeenth century, as a progressive step leading to such developments as liberal democracy, recognition of human rights and advances in medicine. However, the dissociation of the three value spheres has in his view led to the dominance of science – to scientific materialism, which seeks to interpret our inner experiences or art and morals in purely scientific terms. The result is a collapse of the great nest of being so that all questions are approached by studying the bottom level: physics. While science only recognises the outer experiences, Wilber advocates the need to recognise and integrate different sorts of experience, inner and outer, individual and collective. Each sort of experience has its own hierarchy of complexity, and those given by George Ellis relate to external experience. It seems clear that to obtain a satisfactory world view which includes both the results of scientific study and our religious experience, we need to recognise not only the higher levels of complexity but also the different sorts of experience we have. Patricia Williams considers that Quakerism is well placed to do this.

> Quakerism appears as science begins to permeate British culture, so Quakerism borrows from science – the centrality of experience, respect for intuition and reason, communal features, reformist tendencies, and an appreciation of the past without veneration of it. Science and Quakerism also have virtues in common: honesty, patience, humility, peacefulness, and unworldliness. Science and Quakerism reject orthodoxy's trust in authority and ancient truth. Thus, the increasing power of science over the following three centuries strengthens Quakerism whilst weakening orthodoxy (Patricia Williams 2007, p. 141).

If we are to understand how God works in the universe, then we have to make use of our inner experience.

4.1 How God acts in the world

Returning now to a consideration of God's action in the world, the problems we have encountered in understanding how we can act appear to be compounded.

In searching for metaphors to use when talking about God, we alight on the most complex thing we know – the human mind. So God is described as acting as we act, although with much more power and authority. John Polkinghorne has written (1998, p. 1):

> The fundamental content of belief in God is that there is a Mind and Purpose behind the history of the universe.

I am not so sure.

The idea of a Mind behind the history of the universe appears to be a reference to God as a designer. Because the universe seems to be governed by universal laws which can be formulated using mathematics it is suggested that it was designed in this way. I accept that the remarkable effectiveness of mathematics in describing the structure of the physical world says something profound about the nature of the universe. But, as I have already indicated (in §3.3), I have real difficulty with the idea of a designer. For me, God is a Spirit, not a Mind, an all-pervasive creative force at work in the universe. However, the complexities of human consciousness and free will referred to in the previous chapter enrich the value of the human mind as a metaphor for talking about God.

I recall the enthusiasm of one of my school teachers for the then recently published *The phenomenon of man* (1959), in which Pierre Teilhard de Chardin writes of "the within of things": everything has an inner element of spiritual energy which lies dormant until it is set in motion by the increased chemical complexity of the beginnings of life (p. 79); then there is a sudden change of state with the appearance of self-awareness (p. 186). Our self-awareness also appears to bring with it a growing spiritual awareness: an awareness of truth, of good and of beauty; of the all-pervasive creative force at work in the universe, which is God. This awareness is our inner experience and I will explore it further in the next chapter.

So God acts as this creative force at work in the universe. If this is emergent top-down action such as George Ellis describes then presumably the hierarchy with God at the top includes us. "That of God within us" refers to our place in this hierarchy. Our spiritual awareness means that God, this creative force, "the ground of our being" acts through us and indeed anything of value that we do is a reflection of this creative force. These words of Paul Tillich (1962) were quoted by John Robinson in *Honest to God* (1963), a book which created a tremendous stir in my last year at school.

4.2 Ultimate purpose

John Polkinghorne also refers to a "purpose behind the history of the universe". He finds this in the fine-tuning of the universe for life. It seems that it is life which gives meaning to the universe, and in that sense life gives purpose to all those thousands of millions of years when the universe was lifeless. Possibly our lives too will be superseded by something much greater. However, my worry about the notion of purpose is that it suggests that we find meaning in our lives through something they are leading towards, either for the world as a whole or for ourselves as individuals.

I recently saw an advertisement on the back of a Manchester bus for the Alpha course which "explores the Christian faith"; the advert suggested that we ask God, "Is this it?" I presumed that this was intended to imply that the answer from God would be "No", with some reference to a life to come. I wondered if God's answer might be, "What more do you want?" Perhaps we should seek to make the best of what we have rather than hoping for something more. Make the most of the moment.

I am not sure that the concept of "ultimate purpose" has any meaning. People usually see the purpose of any action as lying in its future effect, and many religious people seem to see the existence of God as implying some ultimate purpose: the physical universe exists for some purpose beyond itself. The idea complements the idea that the physical universe has been created by something beyond itself. Our brains appear to be so structured that we cannot avoid looking for causes and effects – which is normally helpful to us. I suspect that in the search for meaning, though, this is the wrong question.

It is not easy to contemplate our lives as merely a period of self-awareness which grows quickly in early childhood and then continues until it declines and comes to an end: *niente*, nothing, silence.[1] Is this it? Assuming that you do not die too early or suffer starvation or major illness through your life, the answer might reasonably be, "What more do you want?" Much of religion is concerned with finding a purpose for our lives in something beyond our physical deaths. This, though, is not something which has ever had any real meaning for me – even though I do not find it easy to contemplate my own death or the death of those close to me.

It may be even harder to contemplate our culture or our species dying. Yet cultures do die: when a language becomes extinct, as happens all too often, the associated culture dies with it. We may explore a dead culture and resurrect some of its creations, but our appreciation of those creations can only be a pale shadow of the original experience. Our planet will die and, even if we are able to move elsewhere, it is probable that eventually there will be nowhere to go and human life will come to an end. Indeed, the second law of thermodynamics apparently means that eventually any other life in the universe will also come to an end.[2]

> All the labours of the ages, all the devotion, all the inspiration, all the noonday brightness of human genius, are destined to extinction.
>
> (Bertrand Russell, *Why I am not a Christian*, quoted in Paul Davies 1994, p. 13.)

I cannot help feeling that our need to see our existence as continuing beyond death arises from the limitations of our experience, trapped in time. Human beings have a tremendous desire to preserve things for ever. Hence we move around the world vainly trying to preserve each moment, taking photographs and making recordings, so that we can re-live it in the future. Sometimes we put more effort into recording the moment than in savouring it.

At the end of 1999, my wife Pamela had a brain haemorrhage and for a few weeks it was unclear whether she would survive. I cannot really contemplate life without Pam, but I learnt from her sudden and unexpected illness the need for us to make the most of each moment we have left together. This has been a great strength to me, as her health has continued to cause problems so that she may not have very long to live. No ultimate purpose does not mean no purpose for the universe or for our own lives. If the meaning in our lives comes from the richness of our existence as social creatures, then our purpose is to maximise this richness of each moment for ourselves and others. It does not matter that, once each moment is passed, it can never be recaptured.

> I too will something make
> And joy in the making;
> Altho' tomorrow it seem
> Like the empty words of a dream
> Remembered on waking.
>
> Robert Bridges, "I love all beauteous things"

It is impossible to capture and preserve the essence of any moment. Think about a musical performance – many of the most profound experiences of my life have been musical performances either as performer or listener. Of course, it *is* possible to record a musical performance, these days to a very high quality, but listening to such a recording only partially captures the experience. And most performances are not recorded. For a musical performance, we rehearse and then we perform – and then it comes to an end: *niente*, silence; the experience is over, never to be recaptured but so often immensely worthwhile.

Our whole lives are the same. We begin our lives as helpless babies and very often end as frail elderly people. In between, we are influenced by and influence other people. For most of us there are times of extreme pleasure and times of extreme pain. We are called to live as best we can although most of us fail lots of the time. A moment of extreme pleasure may come from our relationships with other people, from physical activity, from creative activity, from a mystical experience. At such a moment we might feel a desire that it could last for ever – and sometimes the moment does feel timeless. But then the moment takes its place in eternity, and our consciousness moves on. Remarkably, some of the experiences which stay with us most clearly are quite mundane, an ordinary incident involving a parent or a child, which in the clarity of its recollection becomes a precious moment.

There are other moments of extreme pain when we may be overwhelmed by our own failings – by memories perhaps of how we have let people down – or by our awareness of the suffering in the world. These are moments which we might wish had never taken place, but they too are moments which take their place in eternity.

> We are such stuff
> As dreams are made on; and our little life
> Is rounded with a sleep.
>
> William Shakespeare, *The Tempest*, Act 4, Scene 1.
> Associated by Ralph Vaughan Williams with
> the finale of his Symphony no. 6 in E minor.

In his "Ode on a Grecian Urn", John Keats reflects on the moment captured by the picture on the urn and imagines that moment kept for all eternity: the everyday hopes, joys and sorrows of the people preserved unchanging on the urn. Nobody now knows those people. There is a wonder in holding the moment and a sadness that it will never come again. Every moment we live is potentially anticipated, appreciated and then lost for ever. And every moment takes its place in eternity.

I shall never forget walking home to Cheadle Hulme meeting house from Stepping Hill Hospital through Bramhall Park on a gloriously sunny late August morning following the birth of our younger son Mark. A birth is a moment of transition when the world becomes a different place with new possibilities.

> Beauty is truth, truth beauty, – that is all
> Ye know on earth, and all ye need to know.
>
> John Keats, "Ode on a Grecian Urn".
Set to music by Gustav Holst
in his Choral Symphony.

4.3 Suffering, evil and sin: God's love

This is all very well. However, as I have worked on this chapter, Israel has been bombing Gaza and each day we have watched fresh scenes of horror as people are killed and maimed, and see their families killed and maimed and their homes destroyed.

If we understand God as a creative force at work in the universe and in our lives, and our lives as having meaning through the richness of our experience, what do we make of this suffering inflicted by human beings on each other?

We might be amazed at the complexity of the natural world, but it is hard not to shocked at its brutality. It is not just that, for example, animals hunt each other for food and fight each other for a mate. These actions are an essential component of the natural selection process which led to us. There are even parasitic creatures which can only exist by destroying the host creature or causing it great pain.

If we think of human suffering we can divide it into suffering with "natural" non-human causes and suffering which human beings inflict on each other. For natural suffering we might identify protection or warning mechanisms, such as when we touch something hot; the action of other organisms some of which (for example viruses and bacteria) may only survive because of their actions on us; chemical imbalances in our bodies, causing for example some mental illness; physical deterioration; genetic "faults"; natural events such as volcanoes, earthquakes, flooding, drought; and accidents.

Apart from the protection mechanisms, this is all suffering we might prefer to do without. However, genetic faults and the interaction of different organisms are essential for evolution, and I have already remarked on how catastrophic natural events provide an enormous stimulus to evolution. So this sort of suffering appears to be an inevitable consequence of the way that life evolves.

The difficulty appears to be that these events mean, for many people, the rich experiences I referred to in the previous section are just not an option. For most people, for most of history, finding the necessities of life, food and shelter, has taken most of their energies. Some people suffer hunger, cold or illness through most or all of their lives. However, most people do have opportunities to experience love and some sort of human community. A high proportion of those who do not are in that position because of the actions of other human beings.

If we think of ways in which humans inflict suffering on each other we might identify the following: one person seeking to control another person for the other's benefit, such as a parent punishing a child; one person seeking to control another for their own benefit, as in slavery, or for the benefit of the community, as when a dangerous person is detained, or criminal acts deterred by threats of punishment; one person seeking to make another suffer; gratuitous acts by one person on another; the indifference of one person for another; action or inaction by the community (social exclusion, lack of recognition, loneliness); loss (of another person, of an ability); unrealistic expectations about ourselves; unrealistic expectations about others; and self-inflicted pain.

Some of these are consequences of competition for the necessities of life and so might be seen as a natural development of the competition which takes place in other species. But human ingenuity appears to have taken this to a much more extreme level.

This whole subject was a major theme in Jocelyn Burnell's 1989 Swarthmore Lecture. She offers some approaches to the problem but comments how our understanding of pain and suffering is fragmented and partial. She dismisses the traditional ideas: suffering as punishment from God, suffering as part of God's mysterious purposes, suffering to ennoble us or develop our inner strengths. I have to accept with her that pain and suffering is an essential part of the human condition which appears to be one of the "givens" of this world.

Instead of asking why there is evil in the world we might ask about the origin of good. Until life appeared, the cosmos was amoral: good and evil had no meaning. The initial appearance of life on earth did not immediately change that. However, once consciousness appeared then suffering began. This was presumably the situation with higher animals, for example mammals. The cause of the suffering was usually the animals' protection mechanisms. Whilst we might regret the suffering and indeed find it very distressing, it is not evil; it is the natural order. Once human beings appeared the situation was different since not only are we conscious and self-conscious, but we also have the ability to discern others as self-conscious beings – a capacity which may be nascent in other primates. This means that when we inflict suffering on another, we are able to imagine that suffering, even to take pleasure in it. So we can be evil, we can sin. In becoming self-conscious, we ate from the tree of the knowledge of good and evil. As John Punshon puts it in his 1990 Swarthmore Lecture, "It is the fall which makes us truly human" (p. 46).

The traditional idea of a fall from perfection seems wrong. Before we ate from the tree we were amoral beings; we were ignorant, not perfect. We could not sin but neither could we be virtuous. Eating from the tree gave us knowledge not just of "evil" but also of "good". Once we had eaten from the tree, we could recognise our "original sin", our animal natures.

It is remarkable that out of "nature, red in tooth and claw"[3] – the evolutionary forces which appear so brutal – came altruism. The roots may be in the family or pack life of some higher mammals, but now the long process of evolution has produced human beings who find themselves led to identify with the whole of humanity and with other living creatures.

> Virtue is indeed a grace – or an instinct.... It is something to be taken for granted, drawn on and cherished. It is not something we must struggle to create against the grain of human nature.... It is the instinctive and useful lubricant that is part of our natures. So instead of trying to arrange human institutions in such a way as to reduce human selfishness, perhaps we should be arranging them in such a way as to bring out human virtues.
>
> (Matt Ridley 1997, p. 144)

Our sense of some actions as being right or virtuous, and others as wrong or sinful, is our conscience. Matt Ridley has described how this sense of virtue may have evolved. However, our conscience appears to be reinforced and modified by our spiritual awareness, by a sense of being part of something greater than ourselves – that consciousness of the all-pervasive creative force referred to at the beginning of this chapter. In his 1954 Swarthmore Lecture, Wilhelm Aarek warns us that

> It would...be unwise for ordinary people to be too much preoccupied with mystical experience. ...It is essential to keep in mind that ethical living is a prerequisite for religious experience and super-conscious visions, just as much as a result of them. The real question in human life relates to the ability and will *to live in accordance with the light one has at any given time.* (p. 37)

This should not be taken to mean that "ordinary people" cannot have mystical experiences, just that we should not worry too much if we do not have an overwhelming spiritual experience like that of Paul on the road to Damascus (Acts 9:3–9). The spiritual experiences of most of us are less dramatic than his, but none the less significant.

Of course we often fail to follow the leadings of our conscience and succumb to other pressures. We then have to live with the consequences: remorse, shame and guilt.[4] Mostly our failings come about as a result of weakness; we know what we should do and intend to do it but from fear or laziness do not succeed and fail by default. Other failings result from feelings like greed which are focused on our own comfort, or anger and hate which may result in a desire to hurt others.

A few days ago I attended a performance of Johann Sebastian Bach's *St Matthew Passion*. One of the most moving sections is that which portrays Peter's betrayal of Jesus. Peter insists that he will not betray Jesus, and he really means it – for he cannot imagine such a betrayal. But then, when he experiences the reality of a hostile crowd, he fears the consequences of admitting his association with Jesus and is unable to live up to his good intentions. Jesus knew the weakness of this impetuous man but loved him none the less. He recognised his potential and knew that when it really mattered he would stand up to be counted. Tradition has it that in due course Peter himself was crucified in Rome. Peter might have told himself, on being asked about his association with Jesus, that it would not help Jesus if he acknowledged that involvement, but nevertheless recognised his own failure and weakness and wept, knowing shame and remorse. We identify with him, for this is an experience we have all had.

The Gospel story moves on to the following morning when Jesus was handed over to Pilate, and to Judas' reaction to this event. Unlike Peter, Judas took active steps to betray Jesus, possibly from anger because he felt that Jesus had let him down; possibly also from greed since it was an opportunity to make money. Yet Matthew tells us that Judas, too, felt remorse when he realised that his actions had brought an innocent man to his death. It is not clear to what extent Judas was responsible for what happened but he had clearly colluded with those responsible. He felt that the action he had taken was unforgivable: returning the money, he killed himself.

Of course the scale of these actions is different. We have all acted with Peter and let ourselves down. But also we have all acted in ways which inflict suffering on others, or which are at least careless of the suffering of others. Most of the time we do know how we should act. From time to time we encounter situations in which every possible action seems to lead to difficulties, but even then we usually know that certain options are unacceptable. When we fail to follow our leadings, we suffer from remorse and guilt; in our heart of hearts, our "Real and Deep Self", we are ashamed.

In her 1980 Swarthmore Lecture, Janet Scott writes of how we cope with this:

> When we face our own unworthiness, when we share with others the pain of self-knowledge, the pain of the world's brokenness, we find that at the heart of the darkness, at the profoundest depths of the human anguish, God is already present, already strengthening and comforting, already bearing our cross. (pp. 47–48)

This was Peter's response. He knew that Jesus understood. He knew that Jesus expected him to move on and to learn from the experience of failure. And this he did, becoming a key figure in establishing the church, in particular encouraging its spread beyond the Jewish community. This recovery from failure is certainly God at work in the world. Judas also knew that Jesus understood his failure, but Jesus knew too that Judas' sense of guilt would be too much for him to bear. Judas was unable to respond to God's love since he was unable to face his own unworthiness. Jesus' message is that we should acknowledge our weakness and failings; if we seek to overcome them, we shall find the strength we need.

4.4 Our experience of God

Thus we encounter God through our weakness.

This was true of Jesus. He began his ministry by spending a period in the wilderness reflecting on what he had to do. We might imagine that this was a period of uncertainty and doubt. The Bible describes various temptations, which we might see as indicating his search for a way of avoiding what he must have known was going to be difficult. We can imagine him aware of his weakness, wondering how he could succeed in his ministry in an occupied land. But by the end of the period in the wilderness he felt able to proceed, "armed with the power of the Spirit" (Luke 4:14. Revised English Bible).

For myself, it can be difficult to move beyond the period in the wilderness. Around me I see the beauty of the world and in my daily life I encounter all the richness of human experience, the rewards of relationships with other people, in particular family and friends, and the satisfaction of achieving something: baking a loaf of bread, taking part in a musical performance, giving a well-received lecture course, helping a student to overcome some personal dilemma, solving a mathematical problem, clerking a meeting which appears to go well. But these things are transitory and, underneath, doubt and uncertainty remain and I am conscious of my weakness – and then, beyond that, of something greater than myself which sustains and supports me.

> I saw also that there was an ocean of darkness and death, but an infinite ocean of light and love, which flowed over the ocean of darkness. And in that also I saw the infinite love of God.
>
> George Fox, Journal (1975, p. 19);
> *Quaker faith & practice* §19.03.

This ability to experience God, the Holy Spirit, the Inner Light, has emerged within us from this long process of evolution. It must have been inherent in the universe from the start, for where else would it come from? When we respond to it we become co-creators with God. It might be asked whether this experience is of some objective reality or whether it is just generated by our minds. I shall consider to what extend our experience informs us about reality in the next chapter. However, it may be that all we can say is that this is an experience which human beings have known throughout history.

At last we have reached the discernment of God's presence, the Presence in the Midst – which is what this lecture was supposed to be about!

God's presence

This lecture began by reflecting on our experience of God's presence in meeting for worship. To put this experience in context I found it necessary to reflect on the conclusions of science about the nature of the world, even though these are still tentative and provisional and leave many questions unanswered. I then went on to consider the place of human beings in creation and considered how both we and God can act in the world.

The consideration of ultimate purpose in the last chapter led me to the conclusion that this is found not in some future event but in the experience of each moment. So now I turn to a consideration of how each of us experiences each moment – and in particular how we experience God.

5.1 Our experience of the world around us

In *Oklahoma!* by Richard Rodgers and Oscar Hammerstein, Curly sings "Oh, what a beautiful mornin'" delighting in the world he is experiencing – the "golden haze", and the corn "as high as an elephant's eye".

I am going to start by reflecting on how we experience the world we live in. Throughout our lives we receive information through our eyes, our ears, our sense of touch, our sense of smell. From this information we perceive or discern the world and build up a picture of it. How true is our perception of the world around us?

Consider a rainbow, that beautiful symbol of the everlasting covenant between God and all living things on the earth (Genesis 9:17). When you see a rainbow, where is it? If you and I are standing side by side do we see the same rainbow?

I recall that the high point of my study of A level physics was the physics of the rainbow, and the calculation of the angle between sun and rainbow from the way that water bends light. The rainbow is formed by water drops bending sunlight, with the raindrops acting as a prism because the amount of bending depends on the colour of the light. The rainbow appears as an arc across the sky, for our brains assume that the light has come in a straight line: we see the source of the light in the direction from which it reaches us even though in reality it has come from the sun and is bent towards us by the raindrops. I was really impressed that by the power of pure thought (using mathematics simple enough for me to understand), and by a straightforward experiment to calculate how much water bends light (the "refractive index" of water), it was possible to calculate where a rainbow would appear when the sun shone and the rain fell at the same time.

This suggests that the rainbow is not really there as an objective reality; instead, it is a construct of our brains/minds interpreting the light which enters the eye. In that sense you and I standing side by side will see different rainbows: each of us sees the rainbow constructed by our own brain in response to the particular light rays which enter our eyes. But we can discuss it, commenting on how bright it is and on how striking it is against the dark cloud "behind" it. We can even photograph it. So surely the rainbow *is* real.

Let us turn to something more substantial, perhaps a polished wooden table. We see it as hard and smooth. We can run our fingers over it and it feels smooth. We can lean on it and it feels solid. We picture it in our minds as a certain geometrical shape: for example, a table top is a continuous planar region, often a rectangle. Does the table have an objective reality? Our normal way of checking what something is "really" like is to examine it more closely. If we were do this we would first discover that the table's surface was not continuous and smooth at all. Eventually we would discover that the table was mostly empty space, an array of atoms; then as we delved further into the fine structure of the table it is hard to say what we would find. There we would get down to the elementary subatomic particles which can only adequately be represented by the mysterious wave functions of quantum mechanics – known to us as mathematical abstractions which certainly have no meaning for most people. So the solid, smooth table is also just a construct of our minds based upon outside stimuli: the ones received by our retinas as light enters our eyes, and by the nerves in our fingers as we run them over the table. In fact our experience of the whole physical world is like this: it is a construct within our brain/mind representing the "real" world we live in.

Here is a rather different example. If you listen to a performance of a piece of music, where does it take place? It is made up a series of sounds made by the musicians – but where are the sounds? Are they in the concert hall? No, the hall just contains vibrating air; the sounds are a sensation in our brains created by the experience of the vibrating air. So far this is just a variant of the old riddle, "If a tree falls in a forest and no one is around to hear it, does it make a sound?"

But there is more. Experiencing the piece of music involves interpreting the sounds. You need to listen, not just hear, and you probably need some familiarity either with that piece or with similar pieces. When you hear a passage of music for the first time it may just be a noise, not making any sense at all. The experience a person has of a piece of music reflects all their musical experience. Daniel Dennett (1993, p. 387) compares our experience of listening to one of J.S. Bach's chorale cantatas to the experience of a Leipzig Lutheran churchgoer at the first performance in 1725. Our experience is quite different because of the difference in culture. "Our musical imagination has been enriched and complicated in many ways (by Mozart, by Charlie Parker, by the Beatles), but also it has lost some powerful associations which Bach could count on."

An example of which I am very aware is found in Gustav Holst's suite *The Planets*. "Jupiter, the bringer of jollity" is one of the less successful movements but it does contain the most marvellous tune which, in later life, Holst allowed to be used for the hymn "I vow to thee my country". I would love to hear this tune with innocent ears but sadly it is irrevocably associated with the words of the hymn, which brings back uncomfortable memories of my schooldays when I always felt out of step with the annual November celebration of patriotism and militarism. I can never hear that tune as it was originally intended.

A passage of music is a construct within our brain/mind – and this time it is clear that the construct is a response to stimuli received through our senses, interpreted in the light of memories of previous experiences. The same was true of our previous examples of the rainbow and the table. If we had never seen or heard of a table before, we would have a very different response to the sight and feel of one when encountering it for the first time.

All our experiences of the world are really experiences of models constructed in our brains, models which reflect both the stimuli received and our previous experience. In many cases there is a common understanding of these models and with the help of language they become social constructs. When we refer to a table we are referring not to its particular appearance, since tables may vary enormously, but to an object with a certain function.

We experience other people in the same way. We have a clear sense of the objective reality of someone we know well, but this also is merely a construct in our brain. Even our sense of ourselves is such a construct (these ideas are considered at some length by Douglas Hofstadter in *I am a strange loop*, 2007). I am not denying the objective reality of these things; I am just saying that all we truly know is our response to our experience of the objective reality.

So what of God? As described in the last chapter, we have experiences which we describe as mystical or spiritual – of a force for good, a loving power, a compassionate spirit, a call to action – all of which appear to come from beyond ourselves. These experiences have been recognised in all human societies, and people have found it useful and indeed powerful to understand them as emanating from God, because it provides us with language to talk about them to each other and to learn from others' experiences. Different people use different models for these experiences – other ways of expressing them and of understanding "God" – and this sometimes causes problems in communication. We must learn to respect each other's models.

Learning to recognise these spiritual experiences, the leadings of the holy Spirit, the Inner Light, and sharing them with each other is an important part of our religious life. So I need now to say something about mine.

5.2 Growing up in a Quaker meeting

My parents moved to Blackpool in the 1930s and had been involved in the local Quaker meeting for several years when I was born in 1945, a long awaited and much loved only child. So I have attended meeting regularly for all of my life.

In those days, Blackpool was a flourishing meeting. In my early years there was a children's class but by the time I was about 10 or so, I was the only child attending regularly. Then around that time we had an influx of interested young people from the sixth forms of the local grammar schools, and so a Young Friends group started. From about the age of 12 I started joining in their activities, which were mostly very earnest discussions on topics way above my head – I recall a series on T.S. Eliot's *Four Quartets* and discussions of politics and economics – and I don't think

I said very much. I was pretty shy anyway. But they made me very welcome. A little later I joined in the activities of Preston Monthly Meeting Young Friends and then Lancashire and Cheshire Quarterly Meeting Young Friends.

As a child I stayed in meeting for worship for the first quarter hour. I suspect that the only ministry I heard was the regular reading from the *Advices & Queries* (always by the same elder, who worked systematically through them in the style of those days) and the Yearly Meeting Epistle.

> Take heed, dear Friends, to the promptings of love and truth in your hearts, which are the leadings of the Holy Spirit of God. Resist not His strivings within you. It is His light that shows us our darkness and leads to true repentance. It is God's love that draws us to Him, a redemptive love shown forth in Jesus Christ in all His life and above all on the cross. He is the Way, the Truth, the Life.
>
> *General Advices*, 1931

One of the particular pleasures of being the only child in the meeting, or one of very few, was that I was never seen as "one of the children" but as me, Peter Eccles. In the summer months my parents usually did not get to meeting for worship on a Sunday as they were both involved with the holiday trade: like many families in Blackpool we took in paying guests in the summer which was very hard work for my mother, while my father worked on Blackpool Pleasure Beach. But I recall that I went to meeting on my own – I cannot remember from what age. Friends expected me to play my part in the life of the meeting. There was a monthly Sunday evening Adult School, a programmed meeting with a couple of hymns and a visiting speaker. As quite a young teenager I found myself asked to preside at one of these sessions when a Manchester Friend, David Blamires, came to speak on the subject of "Meister Eckhart, a medieval mystic". One year I was asked to prepare the annual report on "the state of the meeting", which Friends took it in turns to do. At some stage during my teenage years "temporary membership", the status of many children at that time, was abolished and I found myself a member of the Monthly Meeting without really noticing. I certainly felt myself to be part of that community of Friends, although I am not sure whether I would have felt able to apply for membership if that had been expected of me.

My first visit to Friends House (and in fact my first visit to London) was in May 1964 when, at the age of 18, I was sent by Preston Monthly Meeting to the Penal Affairs Conference which led to a request to Meeting for Sufferings[1] to set up a Penal Affairs Committee. I was completely out of my depth at this conference as I knew nothing about penal affairs. I can now remember nothing about it; I had to check the details in *The Friend*. However, it gave me a chance to visit the Royal Festival Hall for the first time. So at 3pm on Sunday 24 May 1964, I sat in the choir seats of the Royal Festival Hall and heard a live string quartet for the first time: the Amadeus String Quartet playing the last completed string quartet by Joseph Haydn. I was bowled over. This was one my lifetime peak experiences. I could not have imagined then that the next time I would be sitting in those choir seats would be 25 years later as a member of a Quaker chorus.

I am immensely grateful to all the Friends of Blackpool Meeting and Preston Monthly Meeting of that time for the community they provided and for the way in which they expected me to play a full part in the life of the meeting. I probably could not then have articulated much of my faith. But I knew the reality of a faithful worshipping community.

5.3 Traditional Christian liturgy

My contact with other churches was more limited. In the Cubs, I was expected to go once a month to church parade in South Shore parish church but, although I enjoyed the singing of the hymns if not the psalms, I found the services incomprehensible. At secondary school the morning assembly was basically Anglican as the headmaster was an Anglican clergyman. I recall that some of the collects from the prayer book were used on occasion and I appreciated the elegance of the language. The head of religious education encouraged some sharing of different traditions, and I remember giving a short talk on "Why I am a Quaker" when I was about 15 – although I cannot imagine what I said. Around this time the headmaster took us for religious education and I recall the pleasure of learning to read the Gospel of Luke as a historical document with all its variety of sources, studying who wrote it, for whom it was written and how it related to the other Gospels. This brought it alive as a document.

During my student days at Cambridge I started attending Clare College Chapel and in particular the Sunday morning communion services. Although I did not normally take the physical elements in the communion my regular attendance at the service helped me to understand something of the power of the liturgy, a regularly repeated pattern of prayer which can underpin the whole of life. The dynamic of the service builds up slowly through "the liturgy of the word" which includes Bible reading and the creed, followed by the confession, absolution and invitation to communion. The sharing of the bread and the wine comes right at the end and then quickly the service is over (once the presiding clergy have done the washing up – I was always struck by this tidy feature of the Anglican communion service) and you are returned to normal life. At college, the left-over bread was shared at breakfast afterwards and I was happy to join in that sharing.

Through the chapel I found myself involved in a group called the Cambridge Pastorate, based on one of the local Anglican churches. I even went with them to take part in a parish mission in Streatham in September 1965. Participating in this group I had to learn to articulate my own faith, and I discovered a great deal about the richness of the Anglican tradition and in particular the meaning of the communion service for most Christians. They were very welcoming to this peculiar Quaker; I recall that they experimented with periods of silent worship in our corporate worship.

I have always attended meeting. Cambridge Meeting (there was only the one, Jesus Lane, in 1964, though the Oast House Meeting started in 1966) and Cambridge Young Friends provided my main spiritual community for the four years I was in Cambridge. Cambridge Young Friends gave me my first experience of clerking, and the Cambridge Student Christian Council, on which I represented Young Friends for a time, provided my first experience of the rather different responsibilities of chairing. But I have always been grateful for the fellowship I found in the college chapel and the Cambridge Pastorate for the first couple of years I was at Cambridge.

The traditional Christian liturgy which I found so powerful when I first encountered it in my student days is one response to our experience of God.

> *Agnus Dei,*
> *Qui tollis peccata mundi,*
> *Dona nobis pacem.*

> Lamb of God,
> Who takes away the sins of the world,
> Give us peace.

There is a power in these words which I cannot deny. They are a response to a world scarred by suffering and evil and express a longing for peace. For me the phrase "Lamb of God" reflects the vulnerability and frailty of God's way, which were demonstrated in the life and death of Jesus. I referred at the end of the previous chapter to our shame when we succumb to our weakness and suppress the leadings of the Spirit. The belief that the Lamb of

God can "take away the sins of the world" is the belief that, in this vulnerability and frailty, if we accept our shame (or in other language, if we repent) then we can find the strength and comfort we need to move forward.

These words never cease to move me. There is a power in words which have been used for hundreds of years. In recent years I have usually encountered them when singing or listening to a concert performance of a setting of the Mass.

Simplicity is difficult when we engage the rich variety of humanity's experience of God which is essentially indescribable, particularly given that the language of God and spirituality is laden with centuries of associated meanings. However, Friends try to express their faith in a simple way and are uncomfortable with the elaborate theology which the church has constructed to provide a framework for our experience of God. Typical of the words we use are the following:

> There is a spirit which I feel that delights to do no evil, nor to revenge any wrong, but delights to endure all things, in hope to enjoy its own in the end.[2]
>
> James Nayler (1660) in
> *Quaker faith & practice* §19.12

These words appear to be an expression of something of the same experience as the *Agnus Dei*. They have a special resonance for us because of what we know of James Nayler's great suffering towards the end of his life.

5.4 Worldwide Quakerism

In 1967 the Fourth World Conference of Friends took place in Greensboro, North Carolina. London Yearly Meeting sent 90 Friends to this event including a representative of each monthly meeting. At a late stage the Friend appointed by Preston Monthly Meeting dropped out and I was appointed to go instead. I had never been out of Britain before.

Associated with the World Conference, the Young Friends of North America had arranged a series of events for Young Friends and so I went to the United States for about eight weeks. Before that summer I knew nothing of Friends in other countries. I learnt so much that summer about Friends and about myself. I had never experienced 900 Friends in one room before the World Conference and although the majority were from the liberal tradition, there were many there from other traditions, Friends who were much more comfortable with traditional religious language.

After the Conference, five of us – an American, a Jamaican, a New Zealander and two of us from Britain – spent three weeks visiting Friends, mainly in North Carolina and Florida. In North Carolina we first went to the small Conservative Yearly Meeting in session, where Friends made us very welcome and which was not so unfamiliar in its ways. Secondly we visited a number of large Friends churches belonging to Friends United Meeting, which were also very welcoming but which were something of a shock for the three of us not from the Americas. These churches employed a pastor and had a "programmed" meeting with an order of service consisting of Bible readings, hymns, spoken prayers and a prepared message, usually given by the pastor but sometimes by us. There was usually a period of open worship rooted in silent waiting but this was often for no more than a few minutes. In addition, this was at the height of the Vietnam war and the draft was a real concern for many young men. Although this was no longer an issue in Britain for my generation, I had grown up in a world where it was accepted that most Quaker men (and some women) had been conscientious objectors. Many of the American Friends I had met in New York and Washington before the World Conference were very active in opposing the war. This was not so true amongst young men in the Friends churches in North Carolina. I wondered what it was that had made these people Quakers. Their form of worship was more or less a free church service, they didn't take so much account of the peace testimony and their religious language was conventionally Christian with a strong emphasis on the Bible. But they clearly felt themselves to be Quakers and could look back to the writings of early Friends, identifying with them as much as I could – although possibly they focused on passages which I might prefer to ignore.

American Quakerism had suffered a number of separations in the nineteenth century for various reasons including differences of doctrine. This was how there came to be the two yearly meetings in North Carolina, the larger one, belonging to the Friends United Meeting, having churches, pastors and programmed meetings, and being strongly grounded in the Bible, the smaller one having meeting houses, traditional unprogrammed meetings and a grounding in the Inner Light. The two groups had had little contact for many years until they came together in planning the World Conference.

Through the twentieth century, younger Friends had taken a lead in bringing groups together. The summer ended with a Young Friends of North America conference in Poughkeepsie, New York. As far as I can remember, this conference was more representative of Friends across the continent than the World Conference had been. Some of the separated yearly meetings had joined together again, starting with the two New England yearly meetings in 1945, but this was still quite recent in 1967.[3] I have three particular memories of the Young Friends conference: a wonderful partially programmed meeting for worship at the end which combined the best of different traditions: the stillness of a gathered meeting, spoken ministry, song and dance; our support for Marge Nelson who was about to go to work in Quang Nai in Vietnam as a doctor; and the box of sweets which was passed round in a business session – remarkably they had been manufactured at the Daintee sweet factory in Blackpool where I had worked as my first summer job a few years earlier!

That summer in North America changed my life in all sorts of ways. I could never again take for granted what Quakerism was, how Quakers worshipped, how Quakers conducted business, or the various testimonies of Quakerism. And, most significantly for me, three years later I married Pamela Goldsbury, the New Zealander in the group visiting Friends in North Carolina and Florida.

For most Friends who were there, the World Conference of 1967 was a once in a lifetime experience. But in 1972 I found myself a representative of London Yearly Meeting on Friends World Committee for Consultation and that involvement continued for nearly 30 years, during which I attended eight triennial meetings of the Committee and was even able to attend another World Conference in 1991. During that time my knowledge and appreciation of the different traditions of Friends increased, while the involvement of Friends from different traditions in the Friends World Committee also strengthened. I have learned to accept and understand that Friends do things in different ways, that each group of Friends has evolved from the early Friends in Britain and that the seeds of the differences between these groups were to some extent alive within the community of early Friends.

Though many Friends around the world are unfamiliar with our form of unprogrammed meeting for worship, most British Friends would probably consider that the experience of the stillness of a gathered meeting is at the heart of their Quakerism. So, having described a little of my religious upbringing I will return to a consideration of this experience.

5.5 The experience of God in meeting for worship

I have never found sitting in the stillness of meeting for worship easy, even though I have attended meeting at least once each week for most of my life. I must have spent well over 3,000 hours sitting in a meeting for worship – that's over four months! I am very undisciplined, my mind easily wanders, I get bored and I have never really developed any good techniques for centring down. I suppose that because it is something I have done all my life, I just take participation in meeting for worship for granted. I often wonder what it is like to attend meeting for the first time. Perhaps it is like my experience of listening to a string quartet for the first time.

That is one way I could look at it: I go to meeting because I have always gone to meeting. However, in spite of my undisciplined approach to meeting for worship I know from past experience that at any moment in meeting I might find myself like T. S. Eliot "at the still point of the turning world", possibly as a result of some spoken ministry which has gathered the meeting or possibly just from the shared experience of stillness and the promptings of the Spirit.

> Wait, wait, wait in the stillness.
> Wait, wait, let the gathering unite.
> Wait, wait, wait in the silence.
> Wait, with the children of the Light.

> Come gently to worlds that are new.
> Surrender yourself and be still.
> Abandon your wisdom and will
> To die in the silence in you.
> At first let your thoughts overflow
> When doubts and distractions persist.
> Don't struggle and try to resist
> But tenderly learn to let go.

> Temptations and troubles appear
> Then sink into that which is pure.
> Submit to the things which are sure
> And all will be hushed and be clear.
> Then that which is evil will melt
> And that which is good be upraised
> And shaken you stand so amazed.
> The kingdom of heaven is felt.

> The light is the love that would free;

It lies as the ground of us all.
It shows that which tempts us to fail.
It heals and allows us to be.
Wait in the Light for the power.
Now wait upon God for his peace.
Deep in the heart it will flower,
Seed ever seeking release.

Alec Davison, set to music by
Tony Biggin in *The Fire and the Hammer*
(*Sing in the Spirit* 2005, 113)

This is a wonderful description of meeting for worship, the experience at the heart of this lecture. We come together in worship on a Sunday morning or at other times in the hope that we shall have this experience. Meeting for worship is nearly always a good experience; the waiting together is good; but occasionally something remarkable happens: time stops and we know the peace of God, the peace that we might have prayed for in the *Agnus Dei* if we had been in a different Christian tradition. This peace gives us reassurance and allows us to set aside our shame, but it also challenges us to be faithful, to be better; to be perfect. We modern British Friends may not be used to the idea of being called to perfection but it was an important part of early Quakerism.[4]

For me at least, this "mountain-top experience" is rare. At the head of his Symphony no. 2 in E flat major, Edward Elgar quotes from Percy Shelley's "Invocation":

Rarely, rarely comest thou, Spirit of Delight!

However, as well as the rare mountain-top experience, there is the less intense but no less important experience of being part of a faithful worshipping group over an extended period. For most of us, this group is the local meeting and I have been so fortunate in those which have provided a home for me through most of

my life, Blackpool and Cheadle Hulme, as well as the four other
meetings I have attended for a period – Cambridge, Wythenshawe
(now South Manchester), Stockport, and Evanston, Illinois. But
it can also be a group coming together regularly for some specific
purpose: a committee, an action group, a body of trustees. The
life of the group may be enriched by the corporate memory of
a shared mountain-top experience. At Cheadle Hulme we all
recalled for many years a moment at Teggs Nose Country Park
near Macclesfield when we spontaneously fell silent for a spell
while having tea on a meeting outing – a collective memory
which deepened the life of the meeting. Or it may just be the
rhythm of coming together in silent worship as well as regularly
"sharing the joys and sorrows of each other's lives" (*Advices &
Queries* §18).

Every person present has a significant rôle in a meeting
for worship. Meeting for worship is primarily an occasion to
recognise and celebrate together the leadings of the Spirit
which each of us knows. The individual in the group shares in a
corporate experience which is rather more than the experience of
an individual sitting quietly alone. An occasional completely silent
meeting may be rewarding, but generally the meeting is helped by
some appropriate spoken ministry. Knowing when to speak is an
example of individual discernment.

The leading to speak in meeting for worship is something that
comes from an inner prompting – one that needs to be tested.
I have to check that it is arises from my sense of the leadings of
the Spirit. I recall when I was a student at Cambridge that I had
never spoken in meeting for worship, apart from reading part of
the Christmas story as one of the children in Blackpool Meeting
as a child. This bothered me. I felt that I ought to be able to do
it. Testing the prompting when I did first speak in meeting one
Sunday morning at Jesus Lane must have been difficult, and it is
possible that the ministry came from my need to break the ice
rather than from a genuine leading.

I still do not speak in meeting for worship very often and am grateful for those Friends in my own local meeting who minister aloud more readily. When I do speak, often the ministry has grown over several weeks; in the first two or three weeks there is the urge to speak but also a sense that this is not the time. Breaking the stillness is so difficult. Patricia Loring (1999, p. 130)refers to the "awesome undertaking to risk breaking the silence of the community's prayer and communion with God … [A]uthentic ministry fulfils the silence of worship rather than breaks it."

Moments of great calm,
Kneeling before an altar
Of wood in a stone church
In summer, waiting for the God
To speak; the air a staircase
For silence; the sun's light
Ringing me, as though I acted
A great rôle. And the audiences
Still; all that close throng
Of spirits waiting, as I,
For the message.
　　　　Prompt me, God;
But not yet. When I speak,
Though it be you who speak
Through me, something is lost.
The meaning is in the waiting.

"Kneeling", by R.S. Thomas (1955)

I am not usually very clear what the message will be when I rise although I may know the first couple of sentences planned and have an idea of the ground to be covered. Ideally the message is lived and felt as it is delivered; the words are not just an echo of an earlier experience. It is important to be constantly asking yourself whether the message is complete.

5.6 Living in God's presence

Meeting for worship is not an end in itself. It needs to be integrated into our daily lives. How do we carry the experience of meeting for worship into every day?

First of all, the meeting for worship should be at the heart of the local meeting community and should transform it into a loving fellowship. We often fall short here. After all, the meeting is made up of people with frailties: this person may appear to be rather bossy, needing to be at the centre of everything; that person may appear not to pull their weight; this person may appear to find it difficult to accept help; that person may appear to talk too much; this person may appear to be unwilling to say anything; that person may appear to criticise everything. If you want a group of people who all get on easily and where there is no friction at all, then probably a Friends' meeting isn't the right place to look. If we are engaging with each other then from time to time tensions or misunderstandings will arise. The challenge is to live with this and help each other maintain the community. If we are resentful of each other, it is difficult to worship together. One of the particular pleasures of a smallish meeting like mine is that everybody knows everybody. I nearly always count the people at meeting (normally under 20) and then think of each Friend who isn't there. After meeting we share news of ourselves and of absent Friends.

It might seem that a group like this would appear rather closed and unwelcoming to someone new. It is true that our meeting changes slowly, with few new faces. But a true community will be open and welcoming so that the stranger is caught up into the fellowship even if only for a short time.

Turning to my life away from meeting, there is a sense in which I can be always aware of the Spirit at work within me and of an inner stillness available to me. This is Reality. At any moment I may find myself in this stillness. But then I may for some time not think at all of this inner Reality, although it is still there. Thomas Kelly writes of living on two levels (1943, pp. 33–34):

There is a way of ordering our mental life on more than one level at once. On one level we may be thinking, discussing, seeing, calculating, meeting all the demands of external affairs. But deep within, behind the scenes, at a profounder level, we may also be in prayer and adoration, song and worship and a gentle receptiveness to divine breathings.

For me, the value of a regular silent grace before a meal is as an act of recollection to this awareness of the Spirit. The more thorough Islamic discipline of praying five times a day which is so important to some of my students presumably has the same function. "Continuously renewed immediacy, not receding memory of the Divine touch, lies at the base of religious living" (Thomas Kelly 1943, p. 30).

Prayer can take place at any time and in any place. Much of this lecture has been planned and prayed over during my daily cycle rides to and from the University, about half an hour each way. However busy I am, these journeys provide times for reflection.

Of course, there are empty times when the immediacy of this inner stillness seems to have vanished. This may be caused by tiredness, by stress, by worry, by fear. You may feel overwhelmed by life's problems and do not know how to cope. Or you may just find yourself in a sterile patch. On these occasions you only have a "receding memory of the Divine touch", which Thomas Kelly said was inadequate. On these occasions you have to be patient. All you can do is to offer your tiredness, your stress, your worry, your fear, your problems or your sterility to God, the creative force which you have experienced.

God's guidance

S o far I have reflected on our awareness of God at work in the world. One response to this is wonder, which is an essential part of worship. However, central to the traditional Christian faith is the idea of a personal God who provides us with guidance, both individually and collectively. This takes us on to what is for many of us the difficult concept of "the will of God".

In this chapter I will explore what we mean by "God's guidance" and "the will of God". Then in the final chapter I will consider the practices Friends have developed to help us discern such guidance and how we act as a result.

6.1 The will of God

We spend our whole lives making choices, about what to do, where to go, what to eat, what to wear and even what to think about. I have already argued that although many of these choices are made without a great deal of conscious thought or even without any, they are real choices for which we are responsible. We do have an element of free will. Of course we do not have a choice about many of the things we do. I cannot stop my heart beating, I cannot stop myself blinking and I cannot stop myself breathing. But there are people who develop remarkable control over even these automatic functions.

Everything we do may have unforeseen consequences, a fact of which we are increasingly aware. The way that we individually, our families, our communities, our species and our planet evolve are all influenced by a vast network of decisions, some major but many of a day-to-day nature, such as our choices of food, of clothes, of how and whether we travel. Many of the major consequences cannot be anticipated. A decision about when to leave home one morning or whether to go to some event may affect whether or not we meet someone. And we can probably all think of chance encounters which have changed our lives. There is sometimes a suggestion that these encounters are preordained, but this seems incompatible with ideas of free will and creativity. In the New Testament and particularly in Matthew's Gospel, Jesus is described as fulfilling Old Testament prophesy and there is evidence that the Gospel was edited to reinforce this view. Understanding this may help to explain some of the material in the Gospel which we find difficult.

Living is a creative activity. Our lives are created by the choices we make, by the choices of others and by events over which we have no control at all. In turn our decisions influence the development of other people's lives. Thus our lives are a communal improvisation. There are times when our choices are very limited and we are mainly dependent on those made by others. When we are young it is some time before we realise that we do have options – which is such an important lesson to learn in our early lives. Our ability to choose gives us power over other people, which children soon learn to exploit.

As we come towards the end of our lives, our choices may again become very limited, possibly as a result of physical or mental frailty. And for many people in the world, lack of food and water may severely restrict the nature of the possibilities available. But apart from the very young and possibly some people with severe disabilities, we all do have choices about how we relate to other people. These day-to-day decisions about relationships may be the most important ones we have to make.

When we talk about God's will, we sometimes imply that

there is a correct decision every time we have to make a choice or at least a major one. This language implies that God knows this correct decision while our task is to discover it. The mystery then is why it is so difficult to determine what this correct decision is. Why is decision-making often so difficult?

In common with many other Friends I am uncomfortable with the idea that God wills us to take a particular course of action; this is not in accordance with my view of how God works in the world. So when we talk about "seeking the will of God" I understand this as indicating the importance we attach to a decision and also the importance we attach to the way we make the decision. If we understand God as a constructive creative force in the universe, then "seeking the will of God" or "praying to be rightly led" describe a process in which we seek so to align ourselves with that creative force which we call God that the decisions we make are constructive and creative. Inspiration may come from outside ourselves, from other people or from inner experience, but in the end the decision is ours. We have to create it.

> We are the music makers,
> And we are the dreamers of dreams.
>> Arthur O'Shaughnessy, "Ode".
>> Set to music by Edward Elgar in *The Music Makers*.

As I pray for guidance in writing this lecture I do not imagine that God has a text ready for me to discover. However, I do believe that there are words that are true to my experience and appropriate for the purpose; if I am centred and open to God's leadings then I will be helped to find these words.

The experience of being led in this way can be profound. Of course most decisions are unimportant, but part of the challenge is to recognise when seemingly unimportant decisions *are* important. Sometimes there is a paradigm shift when something which is taken for granted is recognised as a significant issue. We can see a number of examples in our own Quaker history.

The following incident in John Woolman's *Journal* when he was about 23 and working as a shopkeeper and bookkeeper is well known.

> My employer, having a Negro woman, sold her and directed me to write a bill of sale, the man being waiting who bought her. The thing was sudden, and though the thoughts of writing an instrument of slavery for one of my fellow creatures felt uneasy, yet I remembered I was hired by the year, and it was my master who directed me to do it, and that it was an elderly man, a member of our Society, who bought her; so through weakness I gave way and wrote it, but at the executing it, I was so afflicted in my mind that I said before my master and the Friend that I believed slavekeeping to be a practice inconsistent with the Christian religion. This in some degree abated my uneasiness, yet as often as I reflected seriously upon it I thought I should have been clearer if I had desired to be excused from it as a thing against my conscience, for such it was. And some time after this a young man of our Society spake to me to write an instrument of slavery, he having lately taken a Negro into his house. I told him I was not easy to write it, for though many kept slaves in our Society, as in others, I still believed the practice was not right, and desired to be excused from writing it. I spoke to him in good will, and he told me that keeping slaves was not altogether agreeable to his mind, but that the slave being a gift made to his Wife, he had accepted of her.
>
> (John Woolman 1971, p. 33)

We can learn a lot from this story. This is the first time that slavery is mentioned in the *Journal* but we can infer from the account that, although slavery was then an accepted practice in Pennsylvania even amongst Friends, John Woolman was uncomfortable about it. Possibly he had previously felt that it did not directly concern him. And then suddenly and quite unexpectedly he found himself implicated, with a difficult decision to take at a moment's notice. To have refused to write the bill of sale would have been very difficult and he did not feel able to take such a serious step without more reflection. But he used the opportunity to share his views. Having made a decision with which he was uncomfortable, he did not leave the matter but reflected on what he should have done, so that he would be better prepared if a similar situation arose again. When it did, he was ready to act – although it was an easier decision on this occasion, since he did not have any particular obligation to the person who asked him, apart possibly from the not insignificant obligations of friendship. When he told the man that he was unwilling to write the document he found, possibly to his surprise, that the man was a little embarrassed and had to give an excuse for acquiring the slave. So at each stage the response was creative. From our perspective, the morality of the situation is clear – but we are standing in a place which has only been achieved by the efforts of many, including John Woolman. The seed which began to germinate when John Woolman wrote the bill of sale for the slave led to a plant which bore wonderful fruit in his life and beyond.

If we are to be ready to recognise the significance of what may be quite small decisions then we need to be living in God's presence as described in the last chapter, always open to new leading. This may come in the form of doubts about something we have done. The action may have been more or less instinctive or unthinking; yet reflection on it, reviewing it in the context of the leadings of the Spirit of which we are aware, may lead to a different response next time – as in the case of John Woolman – or may lead to further action – as happened for John Woolman in due course.

I find a parallel here between decision-making in the context of the leadings of the Spirit and the attempt to solve a mathematical problem. In trying to explain to students the idea of constructing a mathematical proof, I find helpful the analogy of finding a route up a mountain. The mountain exists from the start, and your explorations cannot change it. If you find a way up the mountain then it must have been there from the start – constructing the route is really just recognising that route. However, although we are "merely" discovering, or recognizing, the route, this is a creative act. You might come up with a route different from mine. The only criterion in mathematics is that the route follows the rules of logic, the way of truth. When you do mathematical research you may not know what the summit is going to be, and so not only might your route be different from mine but your endpoint might also be slightly different, giving a different view of the surrounding landscape. (This is rather different from the situation of solving a mathematics examination question for which the examiner has normally prepared a "model solution".) When we compare notes, we may be able to extend the route and get a bit further. Indeed, there is corporate learning so that, in both mountaineering and mathematics, routes which were seen as cutting edge and enormously demanding become almost commonplace: hundreds of people now climb Everest; we teach university students mathematical topics which seemed extremely difficult a generation ago; in a different context, pieces of music which were considered unplayable when written are now routinely played.

This analogy may also be helpful when determining choices in living our lives. This time the criterion for the acceptability of a route is that it follows the rules of the Spirit, the way of Truth, and there may be more difficulty in agreeing whether this criterion has been met. I will return to the question of our sources of authority, a matter which has sometimes been problematic for Friends. But sometimes you just seem to know that a route is right. In solving a mathematical problem, on occasion everything suddenly falls into place and you are amazed at the simplicity of it all. (I think I have only experienced this three times when doing original work, but it has quite often happened when I've been studying the work of others.) You know that it is right even before you have checked all the details: it's just like the home straight when finishing a difficult jigsaw when suddenly, after struggling to place every piece, you cannot put the pieces in fast enough. Just as in mathematics, we have to remember that a moment of apparent clarity can sometimes be misguided; we must always be retesting our lifetime decisions. Yet we hope for this clarity in our lifetime choices. There is also corporate learning here. At first people may struggle to follow the lead of the visionary like John Woolman but, in due course, the outcome of choices which seemed very difficult, or possibly were not even acknowledged as choices, become quite clear. Think of our attitude to slavery.

Will we come to a stage where the solutions to dilemmas such as our stewardship of the earth's resources, the resolution of conflicts within and between nations and the fair distribution of resources seem clear? I don't believe that God has a prepared "model solution" to these problems, but God's guidance, or the leadings of the Spirit, provide us with the means to seek a creative response and to assess our own efforts. We may not be able to solve these dilemmas but we can seek to contribute to the solutions.

I used to struggle with the orthodox Christian view that Jesus' life and death somehow transformed the relationship between humanity and God. However, the idea of corporate learning provides a context in which this makes sense. Jesus shows us what is possible. His integrity and love meant that he could accept his own death without hate. And this death helped to transform the way we view the world. It helps us all to be faithful; and we can think of many others who have been led to sacrifice themselves as he did.

6.2 Corporate decision-making: the Quaker business method

The Quaker understanding of God's guidance and its availability to all has had a profound effect on the way we make decisions together. Our decision-making procedures are usually seen as one the distinguishing features of the Religious Society of Friends. Friends operate as a democracy in the sense that the power of decision-making lies with the people as a whole, but not in the sense that everyone has an equal voice.

The principle underlying a system of voting is that everyone's opinion should be accorded the same weight and that the right decision is that favoured by the majority – although when more than two outcomes are possible there are a lot of complications about the precise procedures to be followed, and mathematicians have enjoyed analyzing the effects of using different possibilities. Friends have rejected this way of making decisions for several reasons. We do not even aim for a compromise which will minimise disquiet. We believe that if we are faithful in the corporate search, we can find the right way forward for this group of people at this time.

It may be helpful to review the reasons why we do not follow the majority view since frustrations with the Quaker business method lead from time to time to proposals that a voting system should be adopted at least when we are making day-to-day decisions. This is from our 1931 Discipline:

> In meetings for Church Affairs and on all occasions when matters come to be decided among Friends, the decision should be in accordance with the corporate sense of the meeting and not merely the wishes of the majority.
>
> It is our testimony and our experience that, when we seek it, we receive guidance in all our affairs, but this guidance sometimes requires thought and patience for its full apprehension. If, therefore, Friends find themselves in disagreement, the various views should be stated with frankness and moderation and all should seek renewed guidance that they may be led into unity.
>
> (Church Government 1931, §V.3)

Voting is a very efficient way of making decisions, particularly yes/no decisions. However, it is rejected by Friends for several reasons:

Firstly, voting leads to entrenched positions. Usually most people start with a clear view. The structure of a debate provides for representatives of each point of view to put their case in the hope of persuading people without a definite view to adopt that perspective. There is little possibility that those leading the argument will change their opinions.

Secondly, voting does not encourage a creative response. Creativity requires us to consider seriously the various options and their relationship to each other. Voting encourages people to hold fast to their initial views. Those who are undecided simply have the task of making up their own minds.

Thirdly, the minority, those voting for the losing position, are excluded from the decision. Their opinion does not form part of the decision.

Finally, arising out of this, voting can lead to divisions within the group. It does not encourage a sense of community and mutual respect.

In contrast, the Quaker method of seeking the sense of the meeting has the following features:

Firstly, rhetoric is discouraged. Friends who have been involved in preparing a proposal will be expected to explain that proposal and the reasons behind it, but only in the spirit of giving information. In the same way, someone strongly opposed to a proposal might explain their reasons. However, this is not with the intention of persuading others to agree with them but again is to provide information. Emotion is also discouraged, although it is recognised that people can sometimes be upset by a decision or by the difficulty of reaching one. The meeting will usually uphold someone who is clearly unhappy.

Secondly, we all share the task of seeking the right way forward. This means that we must all try to determine the needs and responsibilities of the meeting at that time and to determine what we are being led to. The emphasis is on the process, everyone present being charged with fulfilling their rôle at each moment: listening to and upholding a Friend who is speaking; seeking to discern the leading behind their words; reflecting during the moments of quiet waiting. In particular, we must each consider carefully whether words we might want to share are needed by the meeting at this moment and are in the Light; and, if speaking, we must keep ourselves grounded so that we only say what is needed.

Thirdly, the final decision involves everybody. This does not mean that everybody agrees with it but everyone should recognise that this is the right decision for the meeting. It is couched in a minute which can acknowledge the views of Friends uncomfortable with the outcome so that they are included in it.

Finally, how we address the issue is more important than the outcome. The primary purpose of the deliberation is to develop a group which can be sensitive to the leadings of the Spirit.

> At its best the Quaker method does not result in compromise. A compromise is not likely to satisfy anyone completely. The objective of the Quaker method is discover Truth which will satisfy everyone more fully than did any position previously held. Each and all can then say "This is what I really wanted, but I did not realise it." To discover what we really want as compared to what at first we think we want we must go below the surface of self-centred desires to the deeper level where the real Self resides. The deepest Self of all is that Self which we share with all others. This is the one Vine of which we are all branches, the Life of God on which our own individual lives are based. To will what God wills is, therefore, to will what we ourselves really want.
>
> (Howard Brinton 2002, p. 133)

> In a sense, the conclusion reached by the assembly is a musical composition, and each participant has one note to contribute; if very many notes are missing, the theme loses its beauty and perhaps becomes unrecognizable.
>
> (Michael J. Sheeran 1983, p. 55)

There is an important distinction between the Friends' way of making decisions by finding the sense of the meeting and decision-making by consensus. The distinction is subtle and I am not sure that I see it as clearly as Barry Morley does in his Pendle Hill Pamphlet. He makes the distinction as follows:

> Consensus is achieved through a process of reasoning in which reasonable people search for a satisfactory decision. But in seeking the sense of the meeting we open ourselves to being guided to perfect resolution in the Light, to a place where we sit in unity in the collective inward Presence. Through consensus we decide it; through sense of the meeting we turn it over, allowing it to be decided.... Consensus is the product of an intellectual process. Sense of the meeting is commitment to faith.
>
> (Barry Morley 1993, p. 5)

He suggests that "the sense of the meeting is a Quaker equivalent of Communion" (p. 24).

I have quite a lot of experience of decision-making by consensus since many university committees normally work in this way. It does have some of the features of the Quaker method described above. Indeed, I consider that the intellectual process of seeking consensus can be a useful part of a Quaker decision-making process, particularly if the process is drawn out over many months and involves different groups. The key to the difference is indicated by the title of Barry Morley's Pendle Hill Pamphlet, **Beyond** *Consensus* (my emphasis). We usually have to move beyond the intellectual. A process which leads to the highest common factor of the participants' starting positions is not going to have the creativity for which we are looking. The greater use of consensus decision-making in the wider community may be a problem for Friends since newcomers do not always appreciate the difference. "The difference between a spiritual approach and a secular one depends primarily on the understandings, attitudes, intentions and openness to the Spirit of those who gather" (Patricia Loring 1999, p. 86).

It is curious that, although the method of decision-making is considered to be such an important part of our corporate life, the histories of Quakerism say very little about its origins or about the details of how meetings for church affairs were conducted in the seventeenth century. The details of the practice vary a great deal around the world, with major differences between the normal practice of Friends in North America and in Britain and Ireland.

I presume that Quaker practice is based on earlier practice by the Seekers, a view supported by Arnold Lloyd:

> It seems most probable that the Quaker procedure was first practised among the Seekers who in their genuine humility "having neither the power nor the gift to go one before another by way of eminency or authority", would provide the ideal training ground for the practice of following the sense of the meeting.
>
> (Arnold Lloyd 1950, p. 24)

One description of a Quaker business meeting is provided by Edward Burrough writing in 1662 about the setting up of the Men's Meeting in London:[1]

> ...being orderly come together, not to spend time with needless, unnecessary and fruitless discourses; but to proceed in the wisdom of God, ...not in the way of the world, as a worldly assembly of men, by hot contests, by seeking to outspeak and over-reach one another in

discourse, as it were controversy between party and party
of men, or two sides violently striving for dominion, in
the way of carrying on some worldly interests for self-
advantage; not deciding affairs by the greater vote, or the
number of men, as the world, who have not the wisdom
and power of God; – that none of this kind of order be
permitted in your meeting. But in the wisdom, love and
fellowship of God, in gravity, patience, meekness, in unity
and concord, submitting one to another in lowliness of
heart, and in the holy Spirit of truth and righteousness, all
things to be carried on, by hearing and determining every
matter coming before you, in love, coolness, gentleness,
and dear unity; – I say, as one only party, all for the Truth of
Christ, and for carrying on the work of the Lord.

> Abram Robinson Barclay (ed.), *Letters, etc., of Early Friends*
> (1841, p. 305); abridged in *Quaker faith & practice*, §2.87.

Jack Dobbs (2006, p. 116) quotes this passage but also refers
(p. 117) to Bristol Men's Meeting in 1669 having a vote to decide
about the choice of new meeting house and its builder, and in
1697 voting on a letter of application to marry from Thomas
Whitehead and Mary Forest. This demonstrates that, even in the
seventeenth century, Friends sometimes had difficulty in reaching
unity when a definite decision was required.

Early Friends considered that the leading of the Spirit, the
Inner Light, was always true: that it was infallible. But there
still remains the question of how we recognise the leadings of
the Spirit correctly either individually or in corporate decision-
making. Michael Sheeran (1983, p. 22) has written that "Spiritual
discernment is the ability to differentiate reliable leadings from
unreliable ones." He goes on to discuss the sources of authority
which Friends have used, including Scripture, consistency with
the Fruits of the Spirit – "But the harvest of the Spirit is love, joy,
peace, patience, kindness, goodness, fidelity, gentleness and

self-control" (Galatians 5:22, Revised English Bible) – and the gathered meeting. To this list I would add previous experience. One of the sources of division which led to the North American separations of the nineteenth century was disagreement about which sources of authority were paramount and, in particular, about the authority of Scripture. Some Friends, influenced by the evangelical revival, considered that the Bible provided the primary authority and that the Inward Light simply helped us to understand Scripture. Others maintained a reliance on the Inward Light, with Scripture providing one way of testing the authenticity of perceived leadings (see Ben Pink Dandelion 2008, pp. 27–28 and 43–44).

Friends' manner of making decisions together is usually considered to be one the most distinctive aspects of Quakerism. It is rooted in our view of the nature of a religious community: how we relate to each other and to God. It is our experience that group decision-making is an act of worship, a time when we come together to be open to God's presence, opening our hearts to God's leadings in ourselves and in others. Members of the group need to be in right relationship with each other and with God in order to make effective decisions.

This applies even to small decisions. If we are deciding when to hold an event –usually a difficult task because every possible time is inconvenient for someone, so that some Friends will inevitably be excluded – then the way we determine the decision matters very much. In a case like this we might even decide to hold the event at a time which suits the majority, but the decision to do this would still need to be a corporate decision made after the manner of Friends.

From time to time major decisions arise. Some of the most difficult are to do with property and money. I can think of several occasions when decisions regarding alterations to a meeting house have proved very difficult. Passions can run high and it may be difficult to maintain the features of our approach that I have described above.

There are particular difficulties at Yearly Meeting level, partly because of the numbers involved and partly because Friends do not know each other so well. On the other hand, since Friends are meeting together for several days there is the opportunity for a real community to grow. At this stage it seems helpful to consider how we have coped with two issues which have severely challenged our Yearly Meeting in recent years. In doing this I am conscious that some Friends were left feeling hurt as a result of each of these matters. I have sought to be tender to this and hope that I have avoided reopening any old wounds.

6.3 Case study 1: Withholding of taxation destined for military purposes

The issue of the right response to taxation for military purposes has been a challenge for Friends through most of my adult life. From the passing of the Military Service Act in January 1916 to the ending of National Service in December 1960, the focus of British Friends' concern about individual involvement in war was conscription for military service.[2] However, for my generation of British Friends conscription was never an issue.

Through the 1960s an awareness grew that the nature of war for Britain had changed. Future wars seemed likely to require fewer people but extremely expensive equipment. This meant that the contribution that most of us made to preparations for war would be through taxation.

In July 1978, Stanley Keeble spoke at Meeting for Sufferings to a minute from Cornwall Monthly Meeting forwarding his concern for the introduction of a Peace Tax. "The personal refusal to fight is not enough, and our payment through taxes for colossal war preparations involves us directly in the responsibility. It is necessary to find a way to refuse to pay for war, and to enable the appropriate share of our tax to be directed to peaceful uses" (Summary of 1978 Meeting for Sufferings in *London Yearly Meeting Proceedings* 1979, pp. 42–43). The proposal was that Friends should take a lead in a campaign for a change in the law to make this possible. Meeting for Sufferings "warmly supported the principle behind the minute and encouraged Cornwall Monthly Meeting together with the Peace and International Relations Committee to continue to explore the possibilities of such a campaign." This led to an extended period of consultation within the Yearly Meeting. In February 1981, Quaker Peace and Service reported to Meeting for Sufferings that while there was general support for the cause from monthly meetings, they "varied in the degree of their enthusiasm" (*London Yearly Meeting Proceedings* 1981, p. 34). Difficulties were seen in using Yearly Meeting funds in support of a political campaign because of our charitable status, and so it was felt best to establish an independent Peace Tax Campaign which could possibly also involve non-Quakers. This was set up later in the year with some support from non-charitable Yearly Meeting funds. This body, now called Conscience: the Peace Tax Campaign, has worked ever since with the support of individual Friends. Its most recent reports indicate steady progress with over 50 Westminster MPs, including the shadow Chancellor of the Exchequer, supporting the campaign.

However, in 1982 the focus of concern on this issue at Yearly Meeting level shifted dramatically. On 12 March 1982, Meeting for Sufferings received a letter "from some 25 members of Friends House staff... asking Meeting for Sufferings, as their employer,[3] to support them in an act of witness by withholding a proportion of Pay As You Earn (PAYE) income tax; the intention being to bring about a change in the law which would allow legal recognition of such conscientious objection."[4] This was the beginning of a very long journey, leading initially to the first of many detailed considerations of this matter by Meeting for Sufferings and Yearly Meeting. The real difficulty was always that because of the PAYE system it was the employer who was responsible for paying the income tax of the employee. However, after a long deliberation, including at one stage a draft minute from the clerk which recorded a definite decision to withhold tax in the following tax year, the meeting recorded support in principle and appointed a group to consider the matter further.

The matter came to Yearly Meeting in May 1983. The large meeting house was packed for the session. The minute concluded as follows:

> Meeting for Sufferings was not asked to approve or disapprove the with-holding of tax as a witness against armaments. Nor is this Meeting asked to express a corporate view on such action. Meeting for Sufferings was asked to make a public witness to the spiritually-rooted Quaker conviction that there do emerge individual conscientious perceptions of Christian obedience that take precedence over the solemn responsibility of Christians to observe secular law.
>
> We recognise the complexity of this subject but are thankful for the expression of our Friends' concern. We would not wish to support a short-term gesture for the purposes of publicity, and are conscious of the burden that a continuing witness would place on Meeting for Sufferings and its members. Some Friends have stops in their minds; we must be tender of these. To pursue the course of action which Meeting for Sufferings is called upon to take might be dangerous and could be a mistake. But we must live adventurously and be prepared to bear the risks and the responsibilities of following the leading of conscience.
>
> We thank Meeting for Sufferings for the depth and wisdom of the deliberations given to this matter so far. We welcome the Meeting's agreement in principle to support the concern. We offer Meeting for Sufferings our prayerful and loving support as they carry this concern forward.
>
> We live in the shadow of death but we also live in the prophetic power of Christ whose spirit guides us.

Following this, Meeting for Sufferings, after two further long deliberations, determined to withhold a proportion of the income tax for those employees who wished to be included, "in order to test the law". This led to the appearance of the 1984 clerk and assistant clerk of Meeting for Sufferings, Beryl Hibbs and Maisie Birmingham, at the Mayor's and City of London County Court on Tuesday 22 January 1985. The judge ordered that the tax be paid. In June the Court of Appeal refused leave to appeal and in September Meeting for Sufferings was informed that the Appeal Committee of the House of Lords had dismissed a petition submitted to it. At this stage Meeting for Sufferings determined that the tax should be paid but that there should be a "new group to consider the ways in which the conscientious stand of the staff could continue to be supported."

This matter continued to exercise Friends. It was considered again by Yearly Meeting in 1987 when the minute included the words, "We are convinced by the Spirit of God to say without any hesitation whatsoever that we must support the right of conscientious objection to paying tax for war purposes." However, Meeting for Sufferings subsequently found great difficulty in finding a way forward. Its report to Yearly Meeting in 1989 included:

> The Meeting was conscious [in October 1988] of its faltering steps in struggling to respond to the challenge of the 1987 Yearly Meeting Minute. Progress would be difficult until the Yearly Meeting vision had been experienced in our local meetings…. The Meeting prayed to be rightly led, as it sought to be faithful to the experience of Yearly Meeting in 1987.
>
> (*London Yearly Meeting Proceedings* 1989, p. 97).

But before Yearly Meeting took place in 1989, Meeting for Sufferings decided in March to withhold tax again. "As we have sought to feel and know our place and service in the world we have experienced a strong leading that we have no alternative but to support our employees as fully as possible, by withholding an appropriate proportion of their income tax." The details of how this would be implemented were as yet unclear. A new group was appointed in May which *The Friend* described as "a wrestling group" rather than a "get on and do it group", for it was clear from monthly meeting minutes received following the March decision that there was a great deal of unease (*The Friend* 1989, p. 591). In July, it was proposed that an appropriate proportion of income tax, representing tax for military purposes, should be withheld and paid to the concerned employees in addition to their net salary. According to legal advice, this constituted "not complying with the law" rather than "breaking the law". However, it became clear that this route was not possible as it offended the consciences of some of the finance staff who felt that they could not give the withheld tax to anybody else, least of all the employee.

In October 1990, Meeting for Sufferings received a proposal that "a way forward might be found by considering our involvement in the use of the wealth of our nation for military purposes because of the requirement in law that we collect income tax from our employees. The meeting united in objecting to our corporate involvement in war preparations as a tax gatherer" (*London Yearly Meeting Proceedings* 1991, pp. 36–37). In due course this led to the decision in September 1991 "to refuse to pay voluntarily that part of the income tax deducted from all our employees' salaries which is attributable to military purposes" (*London Yearly Meeting Proceedings* 1992, p. 37). However, before this action could take place, the meeting learned in November that "some members of Friends House staff felt a strong disquiet about the proposed action and also about the lack of consultation" and so felt unable to move ahead. In December after another long deliberation the meeting "felt unable to continue with its decision of September, and decided that instead the clerk should write each month to the Inland Revenue expressing an objection to the way that PAYE system takes away the opportunity for the expression of individual conscience." The minute included the words:

> Many of us here today and many other Friends will feel a great disappointment that this is all we can do.
>
> We are humbled by the great suffering in the world brought about by the view that war and violence can be a solution to problems. The Spirit of Christ is unchangeable and our inconsistency reflects our failure to hear it properly. Let us seek to deepen our corporate life so that in the future we are more able to discern the action we are called to.

This was my last meeting as clerk of Meeting for Sufferings after seven years at the table, five of them as clerk. At my first meeting at the table we had received the report of Beryl Hibbs' and Maisie Birmingham's court appearance. My last act as clerk was to write the first of the letters which it had been agreed would be sent to the Inland Revenue (see *Quaker faith & practice* §24.19). These continued for some years until in 1993 Yearly Meeting agreed that future action should take the form of a parliamentary campaign undertaken by individual Friends, which was really a return to the approach of the Peace Tax Campaign. The matter came to Yearly Meeting again in 2001 after three members of staff asked Meeting for Sufferings to make representations to the government, in particular referring to the incorporation of the European Convention on Human Rights into British law through the Human Rights Act. With the support of Yearly Meeting such representations were made, but the case was not accepted.

This may appear to be a record of failure. There has been no change in the law. Although we spent so many hours deliberating on this subject it was only rarely we could agree on corporate action. When we did agree some action, there was often an outcry from Friends not involved in the deliberation that the action was too feeble or that it was wrong, revealing a disturbing lack of trust in our processes.

But at the same time this is a record of great faithfulness as
we sought over a 20-year period to uphold Friends who had a
clear sense of personal leading. We learned a great deal about
our responsibilities as employers. There must have been many
occasions for each of us involved when we just wished this concern
would go away; once the law had been tested in the courts, it
proved so very difficult to find a way forward. In 1989 and again in
1991 we decided on a course of action then changed our minds as
more information became available, in both cases relating to the
consciences of members of staff. Eventually the concern subsided
as a major corporate focus for Friends in the Yearly Meeting. But
we are all grateful that individual Friends continue to act on this
concern, just as Friends continue to act corporately and individually
in other ways to express our opposition to the ways of war.

6.4 Case study 2: Affiliation to the Council of Churches for Britain and Ireland

The first case study related to an issue where the corporate body
of Friends needed to consider our responsibilities relating to an
issue of personal concern. As a second example I shall consider
a situation when the corporate body had to make a yes or no
decision. Cases like this requiring a definite decision are often the
most difficult for Friends.

The question of the affiliation of London Yearly Meeting to
the Council of Churches for Britain and Ireland (CCBI) and the
associated national ecumenical bodies for England, Scotland
and Wales was a major issue at two Yearly Meetings, in 1989 at a
residential gathering in Aberdeen and in 1997, again residentially,
this time in Aberystwyth.[5]

The problem for the Yearly Meeting was the basis of
membership of the proposed new body. London Yearly Meeting
had previously been an associate member of the British Council
of Churches (BCC), a form of membership which did not require
acceptance of the basis of membership but which enabled full

participation at all levels. The CCBI came into being as a result
of a six-year Inter-Church Process with the purpose of creating
an ecumenical body which would include the Roman Catholic,
Black-led and Pentecostal churches. These had not been in
membership of the BCC. Friends had been fully involved in the
process and we recognised that most churches would only be able
to join a body which had a basis of membership which we would
regard as credal. The Basis of the CCBI was to be the following:

> The Council of Churches for Britain and Ireland (formerly
> known as the British Council of Churches) is a fellowship
> of churches in the United Kingdom of Great Britain and
> Northern Ireland and in the Republic of Ireland which
> confess the Lord Jesus Christ as God and Saviour according
> to the Scriptures and therefore seek to fulfil their common
> calling to the glory of one God, Father, Son and Holy Spirit.
>
> (*London Yearly Meeting Proceedings*, 1989, p. 51)

Aware of our testimony on creeds, the other churches included
in the clause on membership in the constitution of the CCBI a
second route for acquiring membership, as follows:

> Clause 2(b). A church, which on principle has no credal
> statements in its tradition and therefore cannot formally
> subscribe to the statement of faith in the Basis, may
> nevertheless apply for and be elected to full membership
> provided that it satisfies those member churches which
> subscribe to the Basis that it manifests faith in Christ as
> witnessed to in the Scriptures and is committed to the aims
> and purposes of the new ecumenical body, and that it will
> work in the spirit of the Basis.

There was a clear recommendation to Yearly Meeting from the
Committee on Christian Relationships, forwarded by Meeting
for Sufferings, that we apply to join. However, this was a difficult
matter for Yearly Meeting. Those who had been involved in national

ecumenical affairs were enthusiastic about the opportunities which the new bodies would offer and also acknowledged the "gesture of love" (as Meeting for Sufferings put it in its minute) in offering us Clause 2(b). However, other Friends were concerned that Clause 2(b) fudged the issue. It was not just that we objected to a doctrinal basis in principle. These Friends found it impossible to relate their faith to the language of the Basis or of Clause 2(b). After all, some Friends would not describe themselves as Christians. The Committee on Christian Relationships sought to reassure these Friends by pointing out that Clause 2(b) was an attempt to describe how other churches saw us, not how we saw ourselves. But there was a worry that possibly the other churches did not really know what we were like!

This is not the place to explore the details of this issue further. Here, I am interested in how we handled it. Residential Yearly Meetings have their own particular difficulties: the numbers are larger than usual (usually about a thousand Friends or more), Friends are meeting in unfamiliar surroundings which may present difficulties of seeing and hearing, and many present are unaccustomed to Yearly Meeting, maybe even having limited experience of Friends' decision-making processes given the poor attendance at most local business meetings. At Aberdeen there was the additional complication that since the Music Hall where the sessions were held was in the city centre, some distance from the University where Friends were staying, there was just one three-hour session of Yearly Meeting each afternoon. It was arranged that at an early session of the Yearly Meeting, the CCBI issue would be introduced by a Friend addressing aspects of the proposals about which Friends appeared to be uncertain. Then, before the matter came to the meeting for decision, there were opportunities for Friends to discuss details in interest groups. The whole of the Thursday afternoon session was set aside for a consideration of the matter.

I recall that it was not an easy session. In a meeting of some thousand Friends only a very small proportion are able to make a spoken contribution, so it is likely that many who feel led to speak will not be not called. On this occasion, there was pressure to reach a decision because of the CCBI's timetable. No doubt many Friends arrived with a preferred outcome in mind.

Such circumstances make it hard to reach a good decision. It was difficult for a sense of the meeting to grow. Nevertheless, the decision to apply for membership of CCBI was made and it did seem that the clerk rightly discerned the sense of the meeting. With a yes/no decision there are likely to be some Friends who find the outcome difficult, even if they accept that the sense of the meeting has been rightly discerned. It is always important to acknowledge these Friends in the minute. In this case the minute concluded as follows:

> We realise that joining these bodies cannot of itself give us renewed spiritual strength; that strength comes from elsewhere, and will only be available to us in our meetings and in our work as part of the new bodies if we are attentive to God, and listen faithfully for the leadings of the Spirit.
>
> We recognise that we hold in trust a precious part of God's truth, and that it is our duty to see this talent is not buried but put to good use in God's wider purpose for the Christian Churches. This decision to work more closely with other Christian Churches in no way diminishes the value we place on all Friends, their insights and commitment to the Religious Society of Friends.
>
> It is clear that some Friends still have hesitations. Joining the new bodies is a new step which, through our brokenness, could lead us and our brothers and sisters in the other churches to a closer and more active service for God.
>
> (*London Yearly Meeting Proceedings*, 1989, p. 298)

Some Friends certainly left this meeting unhappy, possibly even feeling that the decision had been forced through. The discipline of letting go our preconceived notions is difficult for all of us. No doubt there were Friends of various views who failed in this regard. The discipline is to seek unity and to be ready to embrace a possible change of view. It was reported in *The Friend* that one Friend who had been very unhappy about the CCBI proposals "did not consider it possible to achieve total unanimity at this time but felt that Friends should accept membership in faith on behalf of all" (*The Friend* 1989, p. 1060), This enabled us to move forward.

In a situation like this it is important what happens next. When a decision has been made about which some people are unhappy, it is important to uphold those bruised Friends. This is difficult when the decision has been made at Yearly Meeting level; we have to trust that Friends will find the support they need in their local meetings.

Our application for membership of the CCBI was accepted at the inauguration of the new body in 1990.[6] A Friend, Christine Davis, was appointed one of the six presidents of the new body. Through this period the Committee on Christian Relationships (CCR) visited local meetings to help them consider the issues involved. The Committee reported to Yearly Meeting in 1991 that "Many Friends are anxious that people in the other churches and beyond should understand the non-credal basis of London Yearly Meeting's membership, and it is up to each of us to ensure that they do. As they are reassured on these points, however, CCR hopes that most Friends are now ready to seize the opportunity of membership to witness to Quaker understandings of Christian discipleship today" (*London Yearly Meeting Proceedings*, 1991, p. 79). In 1992 the Committee reported to Yearly Meeting that "Some Friends remain deeply opposed to London Yearly Meeting's membership of the new ecumenical bodies. The bitterness with which these views have sometimes been expressed has been a great pain to us, and we have continued, when asked, to meet with Friends locally to help us all to come to a better understanding of the issues involved" (*London Yearly Meeting Proceedings*, 1992, pp. 84–85).

In February 1992 Meeting for Sufferings received a monthly

meeting minute requesting reconsideration of the Yearly
Meeting's membership of CCBI but recorded the view that the
proper time for this would be "when we have more experience of
working together". A few months later a general meeting minute
was received "referring to distress and division within our yearly
meeting as a consequence of our membership of CCBI". The
meeting recorded "the need for tender concern for each other and
the need for loving oversight" (*London Yearly Meeting Proceedings*,
1993, pp. 55). In 1993 Meeting for Sufferings agreed that beginning
in 1996 there should be a review of our membership of CCBI
(*London Yearly Meeting Proceedings*, 1994, p. 41). It is interesting
that through this period CCR had been devoting increased time
to interfaith work and in 1994 its name was changed to Quaker
Committee for Christian and Interfaith Relations (CIR).

In 1997, Yearly Meeting received the report of the group set
up by Meeting for Sufferings to review our membership of CCBI,
this time at a residential meeting in Aberystwyth. This report
recommended that Britain Yearly Meeting (as it now was called)
"should remain committed to membership of CCBI" (*Britain
Yearly Meeting Proceedings* 1997, p. 164). However, it noted that
"the present arrangements for our membership of CCBI are
unsatisfactory", observing that "in accepting membership by
[Clause 2(b)] we are subscribing to the Basis and Commitment
and thereby making a credal statement." It was proposed that
we enter into discussion with CCBI about the membership
arrangements. The outcome of Yearly Meeting's deliberation was
that the meeting decided to remain in membership of CCBI "in
spite of the imperfections of the situation". However, the minute
did not go so far as the report in dealing with the hesitations but
simply asked our representatives on CCBI:

> to communicate our sense that their description of us
> disturbs us, and that what they see as an affirmation of faith
> can appear exclusive to others.

One of our testimonies is to seek what lies behind words, the things that go deeper. We feel called to recognise that a preoccupation with the wording of CCBI's Clause 2(b) could lead into relationships where the letter dominates. Instead we will endeavour to live in the spirit which leads us to leave this domination behind and accept our current membership arrangements in the spirit of generosity in which they were given.

(*Britain Yearly Meeting Proceedings* 1997, p. 274)

The hurt remained for some after this session. I was particularly disturbed that when a Friend offered a brilliant parody, "2(b) or not 2(b)", during the entertainment on the last evening of Yearly Meeting, some Friends were offended and saw this as making light of their distress – which nobody had intended. At the time I do not think that I felt that the second consideration by Yearly Meeting had got much further than the first, but reading the minute afresh now it strikes me that Yearly Meeting did move forward on the issue. Subsequently CIR has continued to work closely with local meetings on ecumenical and interfaith issues.

As with the Taxation for Military Purposes issue, here again we see the Yearly Meeting striving to maintain unity in the face of real differences between Friends, more focused in this case because of the yes/no decision involved.

Both of these case studies demonstrate how the search for the leadings of the Spirit is a process which is never complete. In each case, at every stage the meeting was aware of the incompleteness of its position. In any business meeting the task is to discern the way forward for that meeting at that time.

When we seek the sense of the meeting we allow ourselves to be directed to the solution which awaits us. It is a process of surrender to our highest natures, and a recognition that, even though each of us is possessed of light, there is only

one Light. At the end of the process we reside in that Light.
We have allowed ourselves to be led to a transcendent place
of unmistakable harmony, peace, and tender love.

(Barry Morley 1993, p. 12)

However, every decision is provisional because we have to be
open to fresh leadings. This does not meant that decisions can be
constantly questioned. The discipline for the individual Friend is
to accept decisions made on our behalf, either if we are not able
to be present at the meeting or if we are uncomfortable with the
outcome, trusting that the meeting was rightly led. Questioning a
decision or reopening a matter is not something to be done lightly.
If a Friend feels that they have some new leading which will take a
matter forward then this leading needs to be tested carefully before
raising the matter. It is a personal decision which needs to be taken
carefully – a subject which I shall now consider in more detail.

6.5 Personal decision-making

If we accept that we have free will then we go through our lives
making decisions. Most of these are relatively minor such as when
to get up, what to eat for lunch, how to travel to work, how to
greet a neighbour we meet on the street. Many of these decisions
will be taken more or less unthinkingly since it would be very
difficult to function if we had to make a conscious decision about
every action we take.

I have already commented in §3.5 how our decision-making
is affected by our genetic make-up and upbringing. I argued that
there *is* such a thing as free will. In discussing this, Robert Kane
identifies a number of different freedoms (2005, chapter 14).
The basic one is what he calls "The freedom of self-realization"
which is basically the power to do what you want to do, freedom
of action. The others are concerned with your freedom to make
decisions. In particular he distinguishes between "The freedom
of self-determination", that is the ability to take responsibility for

your decisions, and "The freedom of self-formation", that is the freedom to form your own will – to form your own character and motives, making yourself the kind of person you are.

This final freedom seems to be strongly connected to spiritual discipline: to how we respond to our shame and learn to embrace virtue. For example, we have to cultivate within ourselves such an attitude to other people that, when we have to make a rapid decision which leaves us no time for any sort of discernment, our actions are Spirit-led. Our instincts for self-preservation or for care of our children might lead us to violence whereas, if we have trained ourselves in non-violence, our response will be rather different.

Some of our relatively minor day-to-day choices may be taken in the context of bigger and more significant ones. We decide how to travel to work in the context of a decision about whether or not to have a car (so that this becomes one of the options) and where we choose to live (which really determines the range of options we have). The choices of what to eat for lunch is taken in the context of a decision whether or not to be a vegetarian or a vegan, or whether or not to consume foods which have to be transported a long way (which prior decisions again determine the range of options we have). Of course these bigger decisions may or may not be made consciously. I have to confess that I have never really thought about having a car, because I never got round to learning how to drive. In case that makes me seem rather virtuous, I should confess that I have also never really considered whether I ought to be a vegetarian (although I suspect that, if I thought carefully about it, I might decide that I ought to be).

Other decisions clearly require some thought. Some can be very difficult. They may involve everyday occurrences such as when we are stopped in the street and asked for money. I may have made a considered rational decision that giving money in this way is not a good idea and I may have determined a policy on how to respond. But I nearly always find these encounters difficult, partly because I realise that I am making judgements about what is best for somebody else ("maybe he only wants the money to buy a drink and that would not be good for him") and also because I know I am being careful to avoid getting drawn into something I cannot cope with, and for which I do not have time. Jesus always seemed to have time for people, but then he did not have a job, did not seem to worry about any family responsibilities, and in any case did not have much money. He just had time and friendship to offer. The busyness of our lives is a real problem. Most of us could choose to be less busy.

That brings us to decisions about how we spend our time. If we commit too much of our time then we become over-busy and may be unable to respond to the needs of the moment. I have a lot of commitments in my rôle at the University, including my work as director of undergraduate studies in the School of Mathematics. However, I have determined that if a student arrives at my office door in any sort of distress then, if at all possible, I have to sit down and listen to them as if I had all the time in the world. Teaching commitments have to come first so I may have to arrange another time to see them, but if possible this should be the same day. The School has over a thousand undergraduate students, so I cannot know each student. It is therefore important that I take the time to treat each student as an individual when they are in need.

What do you do when you are asked to take on some responsibility? This is a dilemma facing most Friends, for we have lots of tasks that need doing and not a great many people to do them. When you are asked to do something this may present you with three issues: firstly, whether you are capable of doing what you have been asked to do, secondly, whether you have the time to do it and thirdly, whether you are willing to do it. If the request has come from a Quaker nominations committee then that calls for a particular response because of our approach to discernment.

This second decision about time is usually one you do still have to make, because a nominations committee may not be aware of all the commitments you have.

However, if the request has come from a Quaker nominations committee or the equivalent, it is not really your place to worry about the question about your capabilities. That is a responsibility for the committee. So, when I was asked to be Clerk of Meeting for Sufferings, the largest group I had previously clerked being Cambridge Young Friends, I determined that I had to trust the Nominations Committee even though I found it impossible to imagine myself in the rôle. More recently, I was asked to give this Swarthmore Lecture and again thought myself a very odd choice. I did spend the summer of 2006 considering the request, but I had to be confident that the Committee – which after all only makes one appointment each year – would have considered it carefully; and I had to trust their judgement that I had something to say – even though I have had doubts about this almost every day since. In doing a task such as clerking, we learn how to do it by the experience of so doing. But none of us gives the Swarthmore Lecture twice (apart from Rufus Jones).

This approach places a lot of responsibility on the nominations committee. The person approached has to have confidence that they will have done their job properly, seeking to discern prayerfully the potential gifts of the people they are considering and the needs of the task. It is therefore important that the committee takes the time needed to fulfil their responsibility in this way.

Once you have determined that you must trust the nominations committee's judgement about your capabilities and that you can make the time, the answer to the third question is clear. You have to agree to do the task, however alarming it seems.

Finally, there are matters of personal concern, when someone feels a strong inner call to do something – something which may at times be difficult. I do not have any real personal experience of this but I will consider how we support Friends with a sense of personal concern towards the end of the final chapter (§7.6).

CHAPTER 7

Obedience to God

I n this final chapter I turn to a consideration of how we seek
God's guidance both individually and corporately and how
this leads to action.

A few months ago when my work on this lecture was well
advanced, a Friend wrote to *The Friend* querying our use of the
word "discern".

> I often get a queasy turn
> When hearing the Quaker cliché "discern".
> Is it now a touch too crude
> To use "establish", "find", "conclude"?
>
> Kurt Strauss, *The Friend*, 11 July 2008, p. 16.

This little verse articulated something of which I had been
conscious as I worked on the lecture. "Discernment" was not
part of the Quaker vocabulary I grew up with. It does not even
appear in the index of the previous Book of Discipline[1] whereas
in *Quaker faith & practice* the list of entries in the index takes up
several lines. On the other hand, the word is not used explicitly
in every one of the latter entries, and is not completely absent
from the earlier Discipline. The change is that we are much more
conscious of discernment as a process worthy of special mention.
Possibly an earlier generation of British Friends took our way of
making decisions for granted, and so had no need to emphasise a
special word to indicate the process.

The approach to decision-making described in the previous chapter has led us to develop a number of particular practices which I shall now explore.

7.1 Meetings for church affairs

The formal name for Friends' business meetings is "meetings for church affairs", the word "church" referring to the spiritual community of Friends or more widely to all of those seeking to following the leadings of the Spirit. In recent years the practice has developed of referring to them as "meetings for worship for business" in order to emphasise that these meetings are just as much meetings for worship as is the normal weekly meeting for worship.

These meetings provide the framework within which we endeavour to apply the principles of corporate decision-making described in §6.2. We come together in a meeting for worship to seek the leadings of the Spirit. The disciplines which govern our participation in meeting for worship – of listening to others in order to hear how the Spirit is working through them, and of testing our own leadings to speak – apply in these meetings for worship for business.

Reflecting on the Quaker business method, Margaret Heathfield in her 1994 Swarthmore Lecture warns that:

> it is a mistake to try to use our Quaker business method as if it were a kind of magic formula which we can use to lead us to discernment of the will of God, whatever the circumstances. In the long experience of the Quaker tradition, it has worked best when it is rooted in other aspects of our communal life – when people know each other well, and when most people present are familiar with the practice of reading the gathered sense of the Meeting in worship and in business.
>
> (Margaret Heathfield 1994, p. 91–92)

Our state of mind and the degree to which the meeting is

gathered affect our responsiveness to the leadings of the Spirit, God's guidance.

> The man who hath no music in himself,
> Nor is not mov'd with concord of sweet sounds,
> Is fit for treasons, stratagems, and spoils;
> The motions of his spirit are dull as night,
> And his affections dark as Erebus.
> Let no such man be trusted. Mark the music.
>
> William Shakespeare, *The Merchant of Venice*, V.1.
> Set by Ralph Vaughan Williams in the *Serenade to Music*.

This is rather negative but makes the point if we consider what mathematicians call the contrapositive statement. Shakespeare says that lack of music leads to dull spirits and untrustworthy decisions. This is equivalent to saying that if we want bright spirits and trustworthy decisions, then we and our meetings need music – which I am here using as a metaphor indicating an attitude of mind. We need to consider practices which enable our spirits to sing.

So the preparation of each participant is important. In the previous chapter I emphasised the creative aspect of decision-making, which requires each participant to be open to new Light. This asks each participant to arrive with an open mind; but not with an empty mind. If information about the agenda has been circulated in advance it is helpful if participants have read and reflected on it, possibly with the help of discussion with others, whether or not they will be present at the meeting. It can be difficult sometimes not to hope for a particular outcome, but such a leaning must be subservient to the hope that the meeting will be faithful to the leadings of the Spirit.

The preparation of the meeting as a body is important, too. It is enormously helpful if the meeting develops a rich corporate life, worshipping together, "sharing the joys and sorrows of each other's lives" (*Advices & Queries* §18), having fun together, as well as grappling with difficult issues. In her lecture, Margaret Heathfield goes on to refer to the particular problems of Yearly Meeting where we may have difficult matters to consider and yet where we may not know each other well. I acknowledge these difficulties; yet it is also true that during those few days, the Quaker community becomes the focus of all the energy of everyone present. Thus contrariwise I consider that Yearly Meeting in session provides a good illustration of how a rich corporate life can help underpin effective decision-making, particularly when it takes place residentially.

When we have been considering the size of Meeting for Sufferings, there have occasionally been suggestions that possibly the two representatives appointed by most area meetings might attend alternately; some meetings have decided that their representatives should do this. However, if this became the norm it would be much harder for the Meeting to develop the corporate life which is so necessary for its effectiveness.

We come together in the stillness of a meeting for worship before turning after an appropriate period to the business. In a meeting where people have travelled to be together or where they do not know each other well, I welcome the opportunity for Friends to greet their neighbours as they gather, without being too precious about gathering in silence. Communion can be experienced in the gathered silent meeting but it can also build on the sharing of little things with each other as we come together. If Friends are sensitive then the meeting will settle into a still silence as the appointed hour approaches.

Then, during the meeting, it is essential that all present participate. One of our difficulties in inviting people such as representatives of other bodies to attend our meetings, is that there is no rôle for a spectator in a meeting for worship: everyone is a participant. Occasionally, someone refers to what "they" did in a meeting in which they themselves were present, rather than to what "we" did. If someone sees themselves in this way as spectator rather than as participant, the meeting becomes less effective. The participation can be one of prayerful upholding of the meeting, holding the stillness, which may be the contribution of most participants in a large meeting.

Of course, meetings for church affairs vary a great deal. The huddle of a small group which meets over tea to tackle some specific task has a different dynamic from that of a session of Britain Yearly Meeting. A small local meeting may appear to have rather informal business meetings. However, in all cases the underlying approach should be the same.

This all sounds terribly heavy but it need not and should not normally be so. The process is serious but we should not take ourselves too seriously. There can times for laughter and humour, as well as for tears. And at any moment, as in any meeting for worship, we can find that time appears to have stopped. We feel ourselves to be treading on holy ground, in the presence of God.

7.2 The clerk and the minute

Chapter 3 of *Quaker faith & practice* gives a good general description of the way we make decisions. One distinctive feature of our meetings for church affairs, our business meetings, is that we have a clerk rather than a chair or chairman. I believe that this name was used by analogy with a clerk in a court of law (of which early Friends had lots of experience) who records the proceedings rather than directing the proceedings. The difference in the rôles which I have noticed most is that the chair of a meeting has a particular responsibility for the *outcome* of the meeting whereas a clerk's particular responsibility is for its *process*. Indeed, one of the liberating things about being the clerk when a difficult matter is being considered is that you have no responsibility for the outcome!

Because of the distinctive part played by the clerk in Quaker business meetings I shall take some time to explore this rôle, drawing on my own experience. So the next few pages may appear to read like a manual for clerks, a curious conclusion to the lecture. However, like Barry Morley, I see our experience of discerning the sense of the meeting as being central to our corporate life, as the place where we are most aware of the Presence in the Midst. It is important that all participants understand the rôles of the clerk and of the minute in underpinning this experience.

It is our practice that the clerk presides in the meeting, guiding Friends through the business and, in a larger meeting, determining who should speak. However, it seems that early Friends' view was that the holy Spirit presides, while the clerk's rôle is simply that of recording the decisions of the meeting. It does not seem easy to discover the details of how early meetings were conducted.[2] Interestingly, a picture of London Yearly Meeting in session around 1840 shows the clerk, George Stacey, seated in the body of the meeting with many Friends behind him.[3] He has a small desk to work on but otherwise appears to be just one Friend amongst the others. That is very different from the present configuration where the clerk is the focal point of the meeting, able to be seen by and to see everybody. However, spoken contributions in the meeting are not addressed to the clerk, as they would be to a chair, or to any other individual. They are addressed to the meeting as a whole, like spoken ministry in any other meeting for worship.

The clerk has the responsibility for preparing the agenda, usually working with one or more assistant clerks or sometimes, as in the case of Britain Yearly Meeting, with an agenda committee. Margaret Heathfield (1994, p. 94) writes of the clerk needing "the skill of bringing as much as possible of the hidden agenda tactfully into the open", meaning by "hidden agenda" aspects of an issue which are only known to some people. A clerk has many of the opportunities of a conventional chair for manipulating decision-making by withholding information or selecting certain people to speak, but such action would be particularly inappropriate in a Quaker meeting for church affairs. The clerk has a responsibility to encourage the openness of Friends in the meeting and a willingness to face up to and work through conflict. This is only possible if the clerk is open with the meeting and if the meeting trusts the clerk to be open.

The key to the clerking rôle is the minute, as is indicated by the number of references to the minute in the sections of *Quaker faith & practice* on clerking (§3.12 to §3.20). I believe that it is the responsibility for producing a draft minute for the meeting which most of us find most daunting when considering service as a clerk. How will I respond when faced with a blank piece of paper during a difficult item of business? What will I do if a matter has been under consideration for some time, the essence of the meeting is not clear to me but I know that the meeting expects a minute before too long?

There are purists who approach clerking in the trust that the words will always come to them in the meeting. Sometimes the nature of the business means that you have no other option, but I admire the faith of those who feel able always to work this way. Usually the clerk expects to know a fair bit about each item of business beforehand and for me the key to effective clerking is careful preparation. As part of this preparation, I do as much prior drafting as I can, recognising that sometimes such drafting is impossible because of lack of prior information about the agenda item.

I certainly prepare outlines of the matter to be considered which may then form the early part of any minute, although it is important to be careful that this reflects the way the item was actually presented to the meeting before offering the draft minute: it is likely to be necessary to make some adjustments. The clerk has responsibility for ensuring that the matter at hand is properly presented to the meeting, and so if something which the clerk has identified as important information is not referred to in the introduction, then it can be helpful to mention it as clerk –

although this requires care in case the clerk might appear to be trying to influence the outcome.

More controversially, sometimes I also try to prepare drafts of possible outcomes if the matter is one requiring decision. I find it useful to make explicit my own preconceptions about what the outcomes might be, and it can be useful to have phrases ready on the page. This preparation helps to provide many of the words which are needed, while the rest usually come from the meeting. However, it is most important that the clerk be ready to recognise when none of the prepared material is useful. Clerks must never produce the minute of the consideration which they hoped or expected would take place – although the meeting can sometimes usefully be cautiously alerted to what it might have said! The clerk must always remember that the minute is the meeting's.

During the meeting I am always conscious of the minute, noting down phrases articulated in the meeting which may be useful. The words for the minute may not come from what is said in the meeting. Nevertheless, it is important to have some sort of note at the table of each spoken contribution. I still recall my embarrassment when clerking Meeting for Sufferings on one occasion when Friends kept referring back to some wonderfully helpful earlier spoken contribution – and neither I nor the assistant clerk could remember anything of the content of that contribution. I cannot now remember how we dealt with this. It can be best for the clerk to leave detailed note-taking on what is said to the assistant clerk so that the clerk can concentrate on discerning the sense of the meeting as it develops. Much can be gained from looking around the meeting, gauging responses to what is being said.

The chairing rôle of choreographing the spoken contributions presents challenges which vary enormously, depending on the size of the meeting. When I first found myself at the table in Yearly Meeting I had failed to prepare myself mentally for the task of selecting who should speak from the 20 or so Friends on their feet, some of whom I knew and some of whom I didn't. I always found this difficult; sometimes it can be difficult to recognise Friends in a big hall and I recall how at York in 2005 some Friends were called several times during the week even though I had thought that I was calling somebody who had not previously spoken. There can be occasions when the meeting appears to be losing its way and you look for a safe pair of hands – but that doesn't always work, and it is unwise to prejudge the likely helpfulness (or otherwise) of the contribution of a particular Friend. Difficulties which in Britain are more or less unique to Yearly Meeting are that it is not possible for all Friends who feel led to speak to be called by the clerk, and that the clerk does not know many of the Friends in the meeting. Even in Meeting for Sufferings, most Friends who feel led to speak either get the opportunity or recognise that their spoken contribution is no longer needed. In most other meetings the spoken contributions come naturally one at a time.

Britain (previously London) Yearly Meeting has changed a great deal in this regard through my lifetime. I recall that when I first attended Yearly Meeting in the late 1960s the clerk would call several Friends at once to speak in sequence, possibly in order to minimise the time between spoken contributions so that as many Friends as possible could be heard. Then in the 1980s a view developed that Friends were not listening to each other enough and a strict regime was introduced of waiting after each contribution, until the clerk indicated who should next rise to speak. This was to encourage Friends to listen to what was being said rather than thinking about what they wanted to say next, and then in the stillness to reflect on whether they had something to share. This practice has continued although in a slightly more relaxed way. After all, speaking in Yearly Meeting is a pretty daunting experience for most of us. This change in practice means that the number of Friends able to speak may be significantly reduced unless the length of contributions is rather shorter.

In all meetings, a significant rôle for the clerk is to take care of
the conduct of the meeting by ensuring that people do not speak
for too long or too often, that Friends take time to listen to each
other and that the meeting stays centred. There are particular
problems in a very small meeting, such as a small local meeting or
a committee, where the clerk may be expected also to participate
as a normal member, particularly if the matter before the meeting
is contentious; Friends may find it difficult to distinguish between
the clerk's contributions as a member of the meeting and as clerk.

In non-Quaker business meetings the minute is simply a
record of what went on in the meeting. In discussion of Quaker
meetings it is sometimes described in this way, as if there were
a threefold process: deliberation, discernment (draft minute),
decision (agree minute). For straightforward business this is
often the way that it works. However, the *purpose* of the minute
is not to record what is said in the meeting, although often it may
do this. The purpose of the minute is to record the discernment
of the meeting, the guidance of God. As John Punshon puts it,
the meeting should be the servant of the minute rather than the
minute being the servant of the meeting (John Punshon 1987,
p. 97). This is the reason for the particular focus on the minute in
Quaker decision-making. Discernment goes on throughout the
meeting, each Friend being expected to engage with discerning
what the meeting needs from them at each moment: reflecting
on the issues, attentively listening to a spoken contribution,
prayerfully upholding a distressed or angry Friend, questioning
whether they are really called to speak and, if speaking, whether
more words are necessary or whether to stop (which should be
the default option). Such attentiveness is particularly demanded
of the clerk, who has responsibility for helping the meeting find
its way through the business. In my experience, a partial draft
minute at an early stage in the discussion can be a wonderful
way of helping the meeting see what it has to do, and helping the
discussion to move on. It is a way in which the clerk can share

with the meeting where it appears to have got to. It may help some Friends to recognise that their spoken contribution is no longer needed. The early partial draft may or may not form part of the final draft minute, since it may be clear to the meeting once this has been read that this is not where it should end up.

When the stage of presenting a draft minute for agreement is reached, the clerk needs to make this clear. It is usual at this stage not to expect significant new material to be introduced but it is desirable not to be too legalistic: hearing the draft minute may prompt a significant new insight. It is this stage of the meeting which many Friends find frustrating.

The concepts of "good enough" or "serviceable" are useful. Very often when I look back at a minute I have written I cringe at the inelegance of the language and see ways in which it could have been better phrased. This does not really matter. What is important is that the minute makes it clear what action has been agreed (if any) and who is to take this forward. It is important to avoid significant ambiguities and to this end I would recommend keeping sentences fairly short; they tend to grow in the drafting process. However, minutes do not have to be written in polished prose and suggestions for stylistic amendments are not usually appropriate. There are exceptions to this. Many older Friends will recall Robert Hewison, whom I first met on the Yearly Meeting Epistle Drafting Committee in 1969. Robert worked as a senior civil servant and had a wonderful way with words. How often he would rise in Yearly Meeting or Meeting for Sufferings and with a great economy of words would gracefully suggest a replacement for some clumsy and possibly ambiguous passage, a replacement which most certainly was "polished prose". As one Friend said of him, "his counsel on detail so often turned a good draft minute into the right minute, and his remarks were always given with such tenderness to the clerk, and often with gentle humour" (*London Yearly Meeting Proceedings* 1986, p. 215).

This stage of the meeting can easily go wrong. If there is broad acceptance of the minute then many Friends will be ready to move on and may be easily irritated by the apparent nit-picking of others. Friends may be tired if it has been a long meeting. The clerk may be tired. The clerk has to discern the weight to be attached to each contribution on the minute. It can be a big mistake to suggest amendments to the minute in response to each contribution in turn. Taking several fairly quick contributions can be helpful, so that none of them acquires too much importance. I usually find it best to take several contributions, take a bit of time to reflect on them, suggest some amendments to the minute if this seems appropriate, then dig my heels in if I am fairly clear that I have got it right. The meeting has asked you to be clerk and so respects your judgement; you have to have confidence in yourself at this point. You will know straight away if you have made a mistake.

7.3 How to proceed when agreement is difficult

I suppose that so far I have been discussing how the wording of the minute is agreed in a situation where it is recording a consideration of a general topic, such as we often have at Yearly Meeting, or a decision when the overall feeling of the meeting is fairly clear. However, things really become sensitive when the meeting cannot reach agreement on some more specific course of action. The two case studies I presented earlier led to this sort of situation on a number of occasions. Difficulties can arise particularly if a decision has to be made by some specific date either because of outside circumstances or because failure to do so would lead to problems. It may help to remember that what is sought is the right decision for that meeting on that occasion. It can also be useful to try and build on decisions made on a previous occasion rather than starting from scratch, although meetings cannot really be bound by their previous decisions.

Our procedures lay us open to attempts by a small group of Friends or even one Friend to block a decision on the spurious assumption that the meeting cannot proceed without consensus. If this occurs, the only option may be to record a decision to take some action "in spite of the misgivings of some Friends" or some such phrase. The meeting always has to weigh the misgivings of any Friend carefully since they may be pointers to the way forward. But in the end there has to be the option of proceeding in spite of them if that is the "sense of the meeting".

Often it is more complicated than this with a range of views in the meeting. One strength of our practice is that this range of views can be reflected in the minute so that everyone is acknowledged. If the clerk discerns a clear leading for the meeting then a minute is drafted to reflect this. Sometimes discernment is difficult and the clerk has to try out a decision in a minute in order to help the discernment. The clerk needs to be straight with the meeting about which is being done.

On a complex issue or one in which there is a range of views it can be useful to have a "threshing meeting". I first experienced this at New York Yearly Meeting and I believe it to be much more common in North America than in Britain. The idea is to reflect on the issue under consideration with no purpose of coming to a conclusion. It provides an opportunity for sharing views on the matter. Then after an interval, perhaps a day or so at Yearly Meeting but maybe a month or two in a local meeting, the matter is put on the agenda again with a view to making a decision. The threshing session provides an opportunity for sharing doubts and fears about a matter without obstructing a decision. It can be liberating. The time before the second session provides an opportunity for everyone to reflect on the issues so that they are well prepared.

I recall that we used this approach in Yearly Meeting in 2002, my first at the table, when we were considering charitable status, the question of how Friends in Britain related to the civil authorities administering charities. This involved tricky issues about the relationship between monthly meetings and the yearly meeting, and about the way in which the framework of charity law might influence our decision-making procedures. I believe that it worked well on that occasion and provided a good foundation for further consideration of the issues in the subsequent three years.

Sometimes it is just not possible to make a decision. On the whole I have a very poor memory of meetings I have clerked. However, I do recall how before Yearly Meeting in York in 2005, Arrangements Committee put a lot of effort into working with the RECAST[4] and Stewardship Committees on a timetable for considering the RECAST report and interconnected issues of trusteeship. In the end this went for nothing. An enormous amount of time was spent on the report with very little progress. Many Friends, including the RECAST Committee, were disappointed. However, there were issues which Friends needed time to digest and Friends *were* listening to each other. We managed to do enough to establish a clear programme of work for the coming nine months. Then the following year the meeting was able to move forward fairly readily and many of the difficulties appeared to have melted away. The previous year's meeting had to some extent played the rôle of a threshing meeting.

7.4 Managing the business

This brings me to the other main responsibility of the clerk: managing the business.

> There is no justification for wasting precious time in our meetings for church affairs under the excuse or delusion that we may safely do so because it is God's work (*Quaker faith & practice* §3.29).

My experience as a monthly meeting clerk a few years ago brought home to me the need to be absolutely clear why a meeting is being asked to spend time on each item of business. What is the meeting being asked to do? A business item may, I suppose, be "for information", but I am not convinced that a Quaker business meeting is the right forum for sharing information. Sharing a concern, yes, because then the meeting is being challenged as to how it will respond. If the meeting gets entangled with detail the clerk, who is often the Friend most involved with that detail, must be very wary of losing perspective. Such finer points can be crucial but often they are not, and the meeting will usually respond to a suggestion that two or three people sort them out afterwards or in the lunch break. The clerk has the responsibility of helping the meeting to use its time most effectively. My experience is that, once the clerk has gained the respect of the meeting, then the meeting will respond well to suggestions about use of time.

Straightforward business is often dealt with most effectively by simply offering the meeting a draft minute at the start of the consideration. Such minutes can be usefully circulated in advance and can then be dealt with very briskly so long as everyone is content. Other than this I am uneasy about circulating draft minutes at the beginning of or prior to the meeting, particularly if they record something that is to take place in that meeting. It undermines the relationship between the meeting and the minute; the minute is to reflect the experience of the meeting, which cannot be anticipated.

The order of the agenda can have a significant effect on the way the business is handled, which places a great responsibility on the clerk, or the Agenda Committee in the case of Yearly Meeting. One response is to dispense with an ordered agenda. I recall that, during the period 1977–78 when we attended Evanston Meeting in Illinois, this was Friends' practice there. Matters came up as Friends felt led to raise them. I imagine that this could be difficult and lead to poor use of time, but Britain Yearly Meeting's current practice, of consciously agreeing the agenda at the beginning of the meeting, is a good one since it means that the whole meeting is taking responsibility for the agenda.

Clerking can be a daunting prospect but immensely rewarding. I have found small meetings the most difficult, partly because the

clerk may be expected to participate as a member of the meeting
which has the difficulties referred to earlier, but also because the
meetings can so easily degenerate into an informality which does
not leave space for listening. A larger meeting can be easier since
people naturally wait to be called. This is not to say that meetings
should be over-serious; a light touch and even humour in a clerk is
usually appreciated, although care is required and the underlying
seriousness of purpose needs to be upheld.

I have worried in advance about the task of clerking a meeting,
particularly a large one or considering a difficult item of business.
However, once the meeting is under way and I look round the
room at the faces of the Friends present (something I always do
during the period before the business) I know a wonderful sense
of being upheld, knowing that my efforts will be accepted. I am
always reluctant to break the stillness at the start of the meeting to
move to the business – the challenge is to carry that stillness into
the consideration of the business.

Meetings sometimes need to be reminded about the need for
discipline. Responsibility for this is shared with the elders, but my
feeling is that it is best for the elders to advise the clerk outside
the meeting and to uphold the clerk within it. It can be confusing
for Friends, and is likely to be a bit disconcerting for the clerk,
if an elder feels led to discipline another Friend in the meeting,
perhaps for speaking too long or off the point. In my experience
the meeting looks to the clerk to provide that sort of guidance.

7.5 Varieties of practice amongst Friends

So far I have been discussing the procedures for decision-making
amongst Friends in Britain and Ireland, and in those groups which
have grown out of this tradition such as Friends in Australia and
New Zealand, which were within living memory part of London
(now Britain) Yearly Meeting. Most European Friends are also
in this tradition, although cultural differences have led to some
variations of practice.

However, most Friends in the world are in North America or belong to groups – such as most of the Quaker meetings of Africa and Latin America – which have their roots in North American traditions. There are significant differences in practice which have always fascinated me. The major differences in practice relate to the rôle of the clerk and to how the minute is prepared and used. In most North American meetings, the clerking rôle which I have described is normally shared between a presiding clerk and a recording clerk, whose functions are more like those of a traditional chair and secretary.[5] The presiding clerk presides, ensuring that the business is presented to the meeting, calling Friends to speak and discerning where the meeting is getting to. The recording clerk drafts the minute, a task which also involves some discernment. The clerkly discernment rôle is split between the two and the precise balance of responsibility may vary from one meeting to another. In our tradition the clerk and assistant clerk share the discerning rôle, the clerk usually relying quite heavily on the judgement of the assistant clerk, who has the advantage of not being responsible for the conduct of the meeting; nevertheless, it is quite clear where the ultimate responsibility lies.

One consequence of the separation of rôles in the North American system is that it is much harder to use the minute as a tool for helping the meeting to see what it is doing in the way that I have described. Indeed it is not uncommon for the minute to be presented at a later stage, possibly at the end of the meeting or, in a long process such as Yearly Meeting, at the beginning of the next session. Whenever the minute is presented, the practice of which clerk deals with amending the minute appears to vary. The discussion on the minute is more clearly separated from the consideration of the agenda item, particularly when it comes at a later stage in the meeting.[6]

Curiously, the Disciplines of many yearly meetings, such as New York and New England, appear to describe the British

practice even though that practice is unfamiliar to most North
American Friends. Only in very recent editions is there any
reference to the recording clerk. It seems reasonable to suppose
that the practice of having a separate recording clerk began in the
meetings which adopted a programmed form of worship. Possibly,
just as these meetings adopted traditional patterns of worship in
the nineteenth century in response to the expectations of many
of their new members, they also adopted traditional patterns of
decision-making. For example the 1979 Discipline of Northwest
Yearly Meeting, an evangelical yearly meeting with programmed
meetings in the north-western United States, has the following
(p. 92) which indicates something close to non-Quaker business
practice:

> The presiding clerk then announces that, as he gathers
> from the discussion, the will of the church is thus and
> so. Unless objections are raised, the recording clerk then
> formulates a minute embodying the proposition and the
> decision. It is very seldom necessary to take a vote in such
> cases or at any time in a Friends business session…Under
> all circumstances it is to be discouraged.

On the other hand the Philadelphia Yearly Meeting Discipline
in 1972 states that "the clerk presides at the business sessions of
the meeting" and "prepares the minutes of the meeting", even
though all my contacts with Friends from that Yearly Meeting
suggest that separate presiding and recording clerks were accepted
as the norm by that time. After all, even in North Carolina Yearly
Meeting (Conservative) which I attended in 1967, the tradition
of separated rôles seemed well established by then.[7] The fact that
the existence of separate recording clerks is only recognised in
very recent editions of the Discipline of several yearly meetings
where the meetings are predominantly liberal and unprogrammed
suggests that the practice is relatively recent in these yearly
meetings, having spread there from the programmed meetings.

There is an interesting additional sentence in many liberal Disciplines that "any member may offer a substitute minute in exactly the same way as the clerk"; the identical wording in the Disciplines of several yearly meetings suggests that the words go back a long way.

There is another practice which occurs in North America but which is more or less unknown in our tradition. I have mentioned the possibility of recognising in a minute that one or more Friends are uncomfortable with a decision. North American Friends sometimes go much further and record the fact that particular named Friends are "standing aside" from the decision. I have no experience of this in practice but I can see that it might be a useful way of overcoming an impasse. However, it seems contrary to our practice of accepting the discernment of the gathered meeting even if that is contrary to our own leadings. The nearest I have come to such a practice is to produce a minute recording our agreement that a particular group could use our meeting house "in spite of one Friend feeling that they should not". In this case the Friend did accept the decision and so did not stand aside.[8]

Of course the lone uneasy Friend may be the prophetic voice who in due course is recognised as having the truth.

7.6 Personal concerns and clearness meetings

I discussed personal decision-making at the end of the previous chapter. On occasion an individual may feel called to a course of action which is unusual or particularly demanding. In such cases we can say that the person has a "concern", although Friends may today be more reluctant to use the term.

> Many Friends today would experience considerable hesitation in saying that a concern, in the full sense of a God-given imperative, had been laid upon them. But some would find it less difficult to report that they had been conscious of a "leading" or "prompting" to take a particular

action or to speak to a particular person. We have no doubt
that many responses to such experience go unrecorded, and
even unreported except to one or two others: the Friend
involved simply does or does not "follow the leading" or
"heed the prompting". It usually does not seem to her or
him necessary to ask for any confirmation through any
formal procedure for "testing", since this is perceived
as associated only with an *unusual* "call" to action or to
service, where the support, and perhaps the involvement,
of one's meeting or of the Society is seen to be essential.
For such Friends the "usual" is probably perceived as the
natural result of their imperfect endeavour to live their daily
lives under the guidance of the Spirit.

(*The nature and variety of concern* 1986, p. 7).

In such cases it is important to test the leading, to ask the
gathered meeting to confirm that it does appear to be in the
Light, a true leading, before acting. In some cases the practical
support of the meeting may be necessary before the individual
can act, which may probably be the case with most concerns
which meetings now receive. However, our understanding of the
leadings of the Spirit, to which everyone is open, requires that any
such strong sense of call should be tested. After all, our history
is littered with examples of people who believed they had such a
leading but who later appeared to have been mistaken.

While affirming that there is that of God in every person,
[Friends] have been well aware that there is that of a great
many other things in every person as well – the "creaturely"
tendencies to egocentricity and self-will are two. We also
carry other voices within us from our formative experiences
with parents, teachers, peers, and other mediators of the
wider society. Long practice of meditation and prayer
underscores that it's quite possible for even an experienced

person to mistake one of these other voices for
her Guide. Early on, quite discerning people submitted
their leadings to others whose capacity for discernment
they respected – usually informally by letter or a talk.

In discerning a formal leading in ministry to the body of
Friends, it became customary to bring it into the corporate
discernment process of the meeting for business.

(Patricia Loring 1992, p. 7–8)

So the final test of a leading should be the gathered meeting
and not the individual.

The normal procedure is described in chapter 13 of *Quaker
faith & practice*. My main experience of the procedure has been
at Meeting for Sufferings when matters requiring support have
come from monthly meetings. Most of these were for travel in
the ministry, visiting Friends, which came before the meeting
several times in the 1970s. The other occasion I recall was in
March 1989 when Chris Cooke and Brenda Heales brought their
concern to provide spiritual nurture for Friends, which led to the
Appleseed project. The procedure is as follows: the Friend lays
their concern before the meeting, there is a time for questioning
and clarification, then the Friend withdraws while the matter is
considered. If the concern is recognised, the meeting provides
a minute of support. It may provide support in other ways too,
and there follows a continuing responsibility to uphold the
Friend in taking the concern forward. It is to be expected that if a
matter comes to Meeting for Sufferings, there has been a testing
procedure at a local level beforehand.

At the local level it may be difficult for the meeting as a whole
to give adequate consideration to the matter. In such cases it can
be helpful to make use of a clearness committee to advise the
meeting and the Friend. This practice is much more common
in some North American yearly meetings where the original
practice of appointing a clearness committee prior to agreeing to

the solemnisation of a marriage has been broadened to deal with other matters also, including personal concerns (see *Quaker faith & practice* §12.22).

It is encouraging that such clearness committees are becoming more common in our yearly meeting. I was impressed that our older son and daughter-in-law asked their meeting for a meeting for clearness before they decided to get married. This has helped them to feel the continued support of the meeting (see Heather Rowlands and Michael Eccles 2008, p. 30). Such a sense that the meeting has a continuing responsibility for the support of a couple marrying under its care is clearly a much stronger tradition in some North American meetings.

The purpose of a clearness committee is to help the individual with the discernment process. It requires great integrity on the part of all those involved as the group should not "feed back what they think the person wants to hear" (Patricia Loring 1992, p. 22). The aim is to help the individual discern what is needed, so the rôle of other members of the group is to ask questions, not to give advice. What is said within the group must be confidential and any report to the meeting about the outcome must be agreed by the whole committee.

I consider that we have an enormous amount to learn from North American practice in this area. The recent revision of the chapter on membership in *Quaker faith & practice* is moving to using clearness committees when considering applications for membership. Much of the current unease about "the visit" should disappear,[9] since the committee will more clearly be seen as supporting applicants for membership as they test their own perception that the reality of their membership should be recognised.

7.7 Discipleship

The idea that the individual Friend might ask the meeting for support in making important decisions is one reflection of Friends' understanding of discipleship. It was interesting that, when my area meeting was recently considering our draft Governing Document, Friends were uneasy about referring to the "Book of Discipline", preferring to refer to its title *Quaker faith & practice*, suggesting that the book's rôle is descriptive, providing information about Quaker faith and practice, which of course it is – in part. The official term "Book of Discipline" could be taken to suggest that it contains a framework of rules, about which we might feel uncomfortable. In fact, it indicates that the book provides a framework for our discipleship – which it also is.

A disciple is "someone who believes in, and follows, the teachings of another" (*Chambers Pocket Dictionary* 2006). Our corporate discernment processes can only work if they are an expression of our discipleship – our commitment to strive to follow the leadings of the Spirit, in particular as discerned in the gathered meeting – and to support each other in doing this. The "discipline" of the Book of Discipline is one to which we each commit ourselves when we become members of the community of Friends, the Religious Society of Friends; it is a discipline not of rules but of commitment. It can be a hard discipline, for the other disciples can sometimes be hard to live with. But creating a loving community of mutual support as we seek to reach out to the world is what we must all aspire to. It is our experience that in this community we can experience the Holy Spirit at work amongst us.

I began this lecture by reflecting on the experience of meeting for worship, the experience which lies at the heart of our corporate life. I then found it necessary to try to find a way of making sense of this experience and of integrating it into a world-view which I could use with integrity. Modern science presents us with a cosmos of immense age and size compared with the time and space occupied by humanity. The place of humanity and even life in this cosmos is unclear. The process of evolution which has led from the first emergence of life on earth to humanity appears to be brutal and violent. And yet it has led to us, self-aware human creatures who are conscious of making choices and of each other's self-awareness. In spite of this mutual awareness we act in ways which hurt each other or damage the community. But we also experience a Spirit within us and beyond us which shows us that we can overcome this: the Presence in the Midst.

Discernment is how individually and corporately we develop this awareness and determine the actions to which it calls us. The final part of this lecture has reflected on some recent experiences of trying to do this and on some of the methods Friends have developed. It should be clear that I am a passionate advocate of these methods, which are more than just techniques for decision-making but reflect something of our understanding of a community of faith. As Barry Morley says (1993, p. 24), "For a faith that eschews outward ritual, … Quakers possess a powerful one; and it works."

In the end what matters is that we are faithful to our experience of the leadings of the Spirit. The quality of the experience when we come together in meeting for worship depends on each one of us. The Presence in the Midst is always with us, ready to sustain and support us. It calls on each of us to rise above our weakness and live out our true self.

> And whenever we pause, and enter the quiet, and rest in the utter stillness, we can hear that whispering voice calling to us still: never forget the Good, and never forget the True, and never forget the Beautiful, for these are the faces of your own deepest Self, freely shown to you.
>
> (Ken Wilber 1998, p. 218)

Notes

Chapter 1

1 The painting now hangs on the Library staircase at Friends House in London. J. Walter West's obituary of Penrose, in *The Friend* of 15 January 1932, gives the artist's account of how he came to paint the picture: "One beautiful summer day I went over to Jordans, and, quite alone, sat down in the seat from which the picture was painted... I seemed as I contemplated all those who had worshipped there in the past, to be surrounded by them in imagination as if they were gathered there. I pondered on what it was that gave them all their power, for they had power in those bygone times, and then I realised that it was the presence of Christ amongst them – 'The Presence in the Midst.' And I felt *there* was a subject that I ought to paint, however inadequate I felt for the task; and I did feel that it was a very great undertaking." See www.quaker.org.uk/swarthmore-lecture for an image of the painting.

2 *Quaker faith & practice* (2005), §3.02. *Quaker faith & practice* is the current Book of Discipline of Britain Yearly Meeting and was approved by the Yearly Meeting in session in 1994. It is a book of quotations and original writing intended to capture the faith and practice of Friends usually revised about once a generation. Most yearly meetings publish their own book of discipline. The *Advices & Queries* already quoted form §1.02 of *Quaker faith & practice*.

3 These words are often spoken in church before the sermon or message. I shall describe in chapter 5 something of the importance to me of the experience of traditional Christian liturgy.

Chapter 2

1 In the third century BCE Eratosthenes was even able to calculate the size of the earth by comparing the lengths of shadows cast by the sun at different points on the earth's surface. (See Carl Sagan 1983, pp. 25–27.)

2 This is the Latin version of the Arabic name since, as with many other Greek texts, it arrived in medieval Europe as a text in an Arabic translation.

3 In fact the system was much more complicated than this. At that time when the sky was still dark at night everyone would have been familiar with the fact that that the planets do not move at a constant rate against the background of the stars – sometimes some planets appear to reverse direction for a few weeks – and in addition the brightness of the planets varies a great deal. To explain these observations an elaborate system was developed. Each planet moved in a circular orbit known as an epicycle which centred on a point on its celestial sphere; the centre of this circle went along a circle called a deferent around the earth. We see such motion in some funfair rides, such as the Monster on Blackpool Pleasure Beach.

4 We see this model fully worked out in Dante's *Divine Comedy*, in particular the third book, "Paradise". Dante sees the ninth "prime mover" sphere as dividing the universe in half. Beyond that sphere there is a similar structure, with God a remote figure at the centre surrounded by nine rings of angels. So the universe is closed and finite with God and Satan at opposite points. See Mark A. Peterson, "The geometry of Paradise", *The Mathematical Intelligencer*, 30 (2008), pp. 14–19.

5 The importance of accurate observations seems to have been recognised by Arab astronomers, an important contribution towards the development of the scientific method in Europe.

6 An ellipse is the shape you see when you look at a circle from an angle; it is one of the so-called "conic sections" which are the shapes you get by slicing through a circular cone (like an

ice-cream cone) at various angles. Although the Greeks had insisted on circles when discussing planetary motion they had made a very detailed study of conic sections in their geometry, so all the mathematics that Kepler needed was ready for him. This is one of the many examples of mathematics, developed for its own intrinsic beauty, turning out to have significant applications – in this case after nearly two thousand years.

7 He also proposed two other laws of motion describing the speed with which the planets moved. A law in science or a natural law is really just a formulation of how the universe works. In the legal sphere, a law is a statement of how people are required to behave – laws may be broken but usually there are penalties. In contrast to this, a natural law may not be broken: if some behaviour does not follow a natural law, this means either that the law is wrong or incomplete or that there is a failure in the observation. The aim of science is to have simple universal laws. If two alternative laws both fit in with observation then the simplest is considered to be the best ("Occam's Razor"). In the seventeenth century, Kepler's laws were a significant step forward because they gave a simple description of planetary motion which was the same for each planet. These laws paved the way for Newton's laws of motion and law of gravity which were a significant further advance since they governed the motion of everything in the universe: planets and objects on the earth's surface were governed by the same laws.

8 However fast the train is moving, when we drop something it moves with us and the train and falls straight down. This explains why we feel that the earth is at rest even though it is rotating (at about 600 miles an hour at the latitude of Britain) and moving round the sun at about 67,000 miles an hour. In fact these circular motions do affect our experience of gravity but the effect is extremely small and was certainly not detectable in the seventeenth century.

9 The church took the view that the Bible made the situation clear; for example, "Thou hast fixed the earth immovable and firm," (Psalm 93:1) was taken to assert that the earth was fixed and did not move.

10 The book setting out this theory (and much more) is the *Principia* (or *The Mathematical Principles of Natural Philosophy*) published in London in 1687. See Isaac Newton (1995) for a translation into English. Newton wrote "I have not been able to discover the cause of these properties of gravity..., and I frame no hypotheses... it is enough that gravity really does exist, and act according to the laws which we have explained" (Isaac Newton 1995, pp. 442–43). In spite of twentieth-century refinements to the theory of gravitation, the problem of describing a mechanism for gravity remains a fundamental problem for theoretical physics.

11 I imagine that Robert Barclay would have seen mathematics and physics as included in logic and philosophy.

12 This is the so-called "red shift" or Doppler effect arising from relative motion. The analogy with sound is helpful: when an emergency vehicle is moving towards you, the sound pitch (frequency) is raised as the sound waves are compressed; when it moves away the sound pitch is lowered as the sound waves are stretched. For light the lowering of the frequency results in a reddening of the light, the "red shift". The fact that most galaxies are moving away from us does not indicate that we are the centre of the universe. A useful analogy is the surface of an expanding balloon on which all points are moving away from all other points but there is no central point on the surface.

13 The description starts from a very small fraction of a second and an enormous amount happens during the first second. The best known popular accounts of this are Steven Weinberg (1977) and Stephen Hawking (1988).

14 This meant that the universe became transparent to electromagnetic radiation. The cosmic background radiation

first observed in 1965 dates from that time, when the universe had cooled to about 3,000 degrees. We now detect this as minus 270 degrees because the "red shift" resulting from the expansion of the universe lowers the frequency of the radiation; this is reflected in a lowering of the temperature. It is striking that the cosmic background radiation is extremely uniform in whichever direction we look, indicating how uniform was the distribution of matter in the universe at that early stage.

15 The question of how far we can see is a little subtle. It might be imagined that because the universe is "only" 14,000 million years old and light travels at a finite speed we could not possibly see further than 14,000 million light years away – the distance that light travels in 14,000 million years. However, after the objects we see emitted their light they continued to travel away from us and so, according to current understandings of the rate of expansion of the universe since the Big Bang, objects we might observe at a distance of up to 14,000 million light years have now travelled to a distance of up to 47,000 million light years. Estimates vary depending on the assumed rate of expansion.

16 According the current ideas, many aspects of the laws of physics, such as the relative sizes of different forces, were determined in the first split second of the universe's existence by a process known as symmetry-breaking. The detailed structure of these laws is crucial for the universe for the existence of life in the universe. These ideas are considered further in §3.3.

Chapter 3

1 It is striking that Newton considered the possibility of other stars having systems of planets. He was clearly puzzled about why the universal force of gravity did not pull the stars together. In fact the stars in each galaxy are themselves in orbit

around the centre of the galaxy and the expanding universe keeps the galaxies apart, apart from the occasional collision.

2   For example, he did not accept the concept of the Trinity: he saw Jesus as the son of God but subservient to God.

3   See for example *The selfish gene* (1989) and *The blind watchmaker* (2006). Richard Dawkins is a superb expositor of scientific ideas. However, his attacks on religion appear to be based on a very restricted view of religion. I agree with his criticism of "blind faith" (see for example *The selfish gene* pp. 198 and 330–31), but faith does not need to be blind. For me, religious faith is concerned with our inner experiences, while discernment as discussed in this lecture is concerned with how we test the reality of those experiences, a process which complements scientific investigation. The examples which Richard Dawkins gives of faith justifying actions contrary to "decent human feelings" would not pass the discernment process described in Chapter 6.

4   It has been suggested that we are now in the middle of the next major extinction event – called the Holocene Extinction Event – as the current rate of species extinction appears to be much higher than the norm. This appears to be caused, at least in part, by the proliferation of human beings. As well as the impact of a large asteroid or comet, a number of possible causes for the earlier extinction events have been put forward such as volcanic activity and changes in temperature, possibly as a result of continental drift.

5   A full explanation of the fine-tuning problem can be found in Paul Davies (2006).

6   In the introduction to the song, Michael Flanders refers to C.P. Snow's lecture on "the two cultures" in which he suggested that not knowing the second law of thermodynamics is like never having read a Shakespeare play. For a more thorough but readable account of thermodynamics see Peter Atkins (2003), chapter 4, which also begins by referring to C.P. Snow.

7 The concept of entropy was introduced by Rudolph Clausius in 1856 in terms of heat energy and temperature. The precise definition of entropy is difficult but Ludwig Boltzmann in 1872 gave a formulation in terms of the then controversial theory that matter consisted of atoms first put forward by the Quaker, John Dalton, in a lecture in the Royal Institution in 1803. This formulation indicated that entropy is a measure of the amount of disorder in a system – something we all experience.

8 The reader may wonder why the uniform distribution of matter in the early universe is a condition of low entropy whereas the uniform distribution of molecules in a sealed tank of water is a condition of high entropy. The difference is that in the universe the dominant force is gravity and so as entropy increases matter clumps together, as happens when the galaxies are formed. In a tank of water the gravitational attraction between the water molecules is relatively small compared with the effects of the collisions between the molecules. There is a fuller discussion of the remarkably low entropy of the early universe in Roger Penrose (2004, p. 730). I was delighted to discover recently that Roger Penrose is the grandson of James Doyle Penrose who painted *The Presence in the Midst*.

9 For a striking example of how self-organisation can appear in a physical system far from equilibrium see Peter Coveney and Roger Highfield (1990), page 186.

10 See John Barrow (2002, chapter 8) for a discussion of the various anthropic principles. A more extensive study is by John Barrow and Frank Tipler (1986). The so-called weak principle states that as sentient beings we naturally find ourselves living in a location and at a time in the universe at which the conditions are suitable for sentient life. The original strong principle of Brandon Carter is the statement that the universe must be suitable for life.

11 I am not sure whether this is Greenwich Mean Time or Garden of Eden local time.

12 There is a variant of this in which the laws of physics vary in different parts of one single universe. According to this, we are living in a part of the universe, our observable universe, which is fine-tuned for life; other parts, which we cannot observe, are quite different.

13 These scientists consider that even if life does appear, then the evolution of self-conscious intelligence is very unlikely. This means, for example, that if our species were to destroy itself then it is very unlikely that another self-conscious species would evolve on earth in the life-time of the sun – which is at present about half way through its life as a stable star.

14 This is a stronger version of the strong anthropic principle. See for example John D. Barrow (2002), page 164.

15 For an excellent exposition of quantum mechanics, see Bruce Rosenblum and Fred Kuttner (2007). The Copenhagen interpretation of quantum mechanics is discussed in chapter 10.

16 See Daniel C. Dennett (1993, pp. 34–35). Daniel Dennett is as vigorously anti-religion as Richard Dawkins.

17 See Michael O'Shea (2005). Contemplating the size of the physical universe as we did earlier makes us feel very small but in a sense we are medium sized objects in the universe. For example, there are about 10^{28} atoms in the human body – that is, 1 followed by 28 zeros – while there are "only" about 10^{22} stars in the observable universe. That means that there are about a million atoms in each human body for each star in the observable universe!

18 Daniel Dennett and Douglas Hofstadter seem to take the view that we can view the brain as a computer, with consciousness arising from the complexity of the programming, whereas John Searle considers that consciousness comes from the particular way in which the brain functions; however, we do not know "how the neurobiological processes in the brain cause our subjective states of awareness or sentience; how exactly these states are realised in the brain structures; and how exactly

consciousness functions in the overall economy of the brain and therefore how it functions in our lives generally."

19 There is actually a third problem: the future may be determined but may be non-computable which means that even if we could know the present state of the system with complete accuracy there would in principle be no way of calculating the future state of the system. Roger Penrose (1989, p. 220) suggests that this may be an essential ingredient in understanding free will.

20 See George Ellis, *Faith, hope and doubt in times of uncertainty* (2004) and George Ellis, *Science in faith and hope* (2008) for accounts of this directed at Friends; and Nancey Murphy and George F.R. Ellis, *On the moral nature of the universe* (1996) for a more extended account.

Chapter 4

1 Niente, Italian for "nothing", comes at the end of most of Ralph Vaughan Williams' symphonies. The music ends in stillness, and then there is silence (nothing) during which we can contemplate the totality of the experience of the piece.

2 See for example Paul Davies (1994). This is the so-called "heat death" when maximum disorder (entropy) has been achieved. Some scientists have considered ways in which life could evolve so that it would go on for ever. See for example the idea of the "Omega point" described in John Barrow and Frank Tipler (1986, chapter 10).

3 The phrase comes from Alfred Tennyson, "In memoriam A.H.H.", Canto 56.

4 I found the discussion of this in Wilhelm Aarek (1954, pp. 39–46), most helpful. He sees "remorse" as the sense of having neglected our duty, "shame" as a feeling of unfavourable appearance to others as a result of anti-social action, and "guilt" as a sense of sin or personal failure. I am not convinced that the words are used to make these distinctions but the distinctions are useful.

Chapter 5

1 Meeting for Sufferings is the standing representative meeting of the Religious Society of Friends in Britain made up mainly of Friends nominated by area (formerly monthly) meetings.

2 It has been pointed out to me that to understand fully James Nayler's words we have to understand the idiom of the day. However, my intention here is to focus on the way we respond to and use these words. As with the Peace Testimony (*Quaker faith & practice*, §24.04) we have taken over these words to express an experience which is ours.

3 See for example Edwin B. Bronner (1966), which I had read as part of my preparation for the World Conference, or Ben Pink Dandelion (2008).

4 For example George Fox (1975), page 27: "I knew nothing but pureness, and innocency, and righteousness, being renewed up into the image of God by Christ Jesus, so that I say I was come up into the state of Adam which he was in before he fell." Margery Post Abbott (1997) gives a varied anthology of Quaker writings on this theme.

Chapter 6

1 The Men's Meeting began around 1656 and was held once a fortnight or once a month to consider the provision of meeting places, the care of the poor and the sick, and the provision of employment for servants losing their jobs because they had become Friends (see William C. Braithwaite 1955, p. 320).

2 There was no conscription in Britain from 1920 to the passing of the Military Training Act in May 1939.

3 Meeting for Sufferings was the trustee body for London (now Britain) Yearly Meeting at this time and so was the employing body. Following the decisions of Yearly Meeting in 2005, the Yearly Meeting now has a separate body of trustees which acts as employer.

4 The proposal was that the withheld tax should be paid into a separate interest-bearing account. This fund would be paid to the Inland Revenue when an assurance was received that it would be used for non-military purposes. See *The Friend* (1982, p. 299).

5 The Council of Churches for Britain and Ireland was renamed Churches Together in Britain and Ireland (CTBI) in 1999.

6 The representatives of the other churches who met with a group of Friends to consider the application reported in part that "we discerned in those we met, and through the practices and publications to which they referred, a coherence manifest in their patterns and traditions which, allied to their emphasis on the person of Jesus, on the dynamic of the Spirit and on their obedient discipleship, constituted a sufficient, if perhaps incomplete, basis in belief and practice for their application for membership under paragraph 2(b), and the mutual commitment that goes with it, to be acceptable." (See *Britain Yearly Meeting Proceedings* 1997, pages 167–68).

Chapter 7

1 This was issued in two volumes: *Christian Faith and Practice* (1960) and *Church Government* (1968).

2 I am grateful to Edward Milligan for a discussion about this.

3 This picture by Samuel Lucas in reproduced in London Yearly Meeting during 250 years (1919).

4 The working group on Representation, Communication and Accountability in our Structures.

5 This is a different rôle from that of the Recording Clerk in Britain Yearly Meeting, whose title describes the responsibility for maintaining the records of the Yearly Meeting. From the first meeting of what became known as London Yearly Meeting in 1668 up to 1703 there was no Yearly Meeting Clerk and the Recording Clerk acted as the recorder of decisions. See *London Yearly Meeting during 250 years* (1919), p. 125.

6 I am grateful to Thomas Hamm of Earlham College for an exchange of emails on this subject. He suggests that on occasions a presiding clerk may offer a draft minute in order to advance a discussion rather than as an expression of the sense of the meeting.

7 However, a recording clerk of North Carolina Yearly Meeting indicates that "the office of recording clerk itself is a fairly recent creation" (Damon Hickey 1987, p. 1). In this book he writes that he is very much in favour of minutes written and read in the meeting which produced them rather than at the beginning of the next meeting even though "this is not common practice" which indicates that minutes are definitely not used in these meetings in the way that I describe.

8 The matter was considered over two meetings and, by the time we had reached this agreement, the group had found somewhere else to meet!

9 There has been a recent change to chapter 11 of *Quaker faith & practice*, encouraging processes more on the lines of clearness meetings (2009 edition §11.11). When an area meeting receives an application for membership it has in the past normally appointed two Friends to visit the applicant. Although the former §11.13 (2005 ed.) made it clear that the visit should not "be undertaken in a spirit of examination" it has been quite common for applicants for membership to refer to the visit as "the interview" and to imagine that its purpose was for the visitors to reach a judgement about the suitability of the applicant for admission to membership. My own area meeting now expects the report of a visit to be signed by the visited applicant as well as by the visitors so that it is clearly seen as a report by all three on the shared experience of the visit. Previously, the report was normally not even seen by the visited applicant.

Bibliography

Wilhelm Aarek, *From loneliness to fellowship* (Swarthmore Lecture), George Allen and Unwin, London, 1954

Margery Post Abbott (editor), *A certain kind of perfection,* Pendle Hill Publications, Wallingford Pennsylvania, 1997

Advices & Queries, Britain Yearly Meeting, 1995; also in *Quaker faith & practice*

Michael Allaby and James Lovelock, *The great extinction,* Martin Secker & Warburg, London, 1983

Beth Allen, *Ground and spring: foundations of Quaker discipleship* (Swarthmore Lecture), Quaker Books, London, 2007

Peter Atkins, *Galileo's finger,* Oxford University Press, Oxford, 2003

Abram Rawlinson Barclay (ed.), *Letters, etc., of early Friends,* Harvey and Darton, London, 1841

John D. Barrow and Frank J. Tipler, *The anthropic cosmological principle,* Oxford University Press, Oxford, 1986

John D. Barrow, *The constants of nature: from alpha to omega,* Jonathan Cape, London, 2002

William C. Braithwaite, *The beginnings of Quakerism,* 2nd edition revised by Henry J. Cadbury, Cambridge University Press, London, 1955

Howard H. Brinton, *Friends for 350 years,* Pendle Hill Publications, Wallingford, PA, 2002

Britain Yearly Meeting Proceedings (Minutes and other documents of the Yearly Meeting; see also London Yearly Meeting)

Edwin B. Bronner (ed.), *American Quakers today,* Friends World Committee, Philadelphia, 1966

Robins Burling, *The talking ape,* Oxford University Press, Oxford, 2005

S. Jocelyn Burnell, *Broken for life* (Swarthmore Lecture), Quaker Home Service, London, 1989

Christian faith and practice in the experience of the Society of Friends, London Yearly Meeting of the Religious Society of Friends, 1960

Church government, London Yearly Meeting of the Religious Society of Friends, 1968

Peter Coveney and Roger Highfield, *The arrow of time,* W.H. Allen, London, 1990

Ben Pink Dandelion, *The Quakers: a very short introduction,* Oxford University Press, Oxford, 2008

Paul Davies, *The last three minutes: conjectures about the ultimate effect of the universe,* Weidenfeld & Nicolson, London, 1994

Paul Davies, *The Goldilocks enigma,* Allen Lane, London, 2006

Christine A.M. Davis, *Minding the future* (Swarthmore Lecture), Quaker Books, London, 2008

Richard Dawkins, *The selfish gene,* Oxford University Press, Oxford, 2nd edition 1989

Richard Dawkins, *The blind watchmaker,* Penguin Books, London, 2nd edition 2006

Daniel C. Dennett, *Consciousness explained,* Penguin, London, 1993

René Descartes, *The Philosophical Writings I,* trans. John Cottingham, Robert Stoothoff and Dugald Murdoch, Cambridge University Press, Cambridge, 1985

Jack P.B. Dobbs, *Authority and the early Quakers,* Martin Hartog, Frenchay, South Gloucestershire, 2006

A. Vibert Douglas, *The life of Arthur Stanley Eddington,* Thomas Nelson and Sons, Edinburgh, 1956

John Eccles, *The brain and the unity of conscious experience,* Cambridge University Press, London, 1965

Arthur Stanley Eddington, *Science and the unseen world* (Swarthmore Lecture), George Allen and Unwin, London, 1929; reprinted Quaker Books, London, 2007

T.S. Eliot, *The complete poems and plays,* Faber and Faber, London, 1969

George Ellis, *Science in faith and hope: an interaction,* Quaker Books, London, 2004

George Ellis, *Faith, hope and doubt in times of uncertainty: combining the realms of scientific and spiritual inquiry* (James Backhouse Lecture), Religious Society of Friends (Quakers) in Australia, 2008

Richard Feynman, *The character of physical law,* MIT Press, 1967

Michael Flanders and Donald Swann, *At the drop of another hat,* performed at the Haymarket Theatre, London, 1963

George Fox, *The Journal,* ed. John L. Nickalls, London Yearly Meeting of the Religious Society of Friends, London, 1975

Galileo Galilei, *Dialogue concerning the two chief world systems – Ptolemaic and Copernican,* trans. Stillman Drake, University of California Press, London, 1967

General Advices, in *Church Government,* Friends' Book Centre, London, 1931

James Gleick, *Chaos: making a new science,* Sphere Books, London, 1987

Chris Gosden, *Prehistory: a very short introduction,* Oxford University Press, Oxford, 2003

Stephen Hawking, *A brief history of time,* Transworld Publishers, London, 1988

Margaret Heathfield, *Being together: our corporate life in the Religious Society of Friends* (Swarthmore Lecture), Quaker Home Service and Woodbrooke College, London, 1994

Damon D. Hickey, *Unforeseen joy: serving a Friends meeting as recording clerk,* North Carolina Yearly Meeting of Friends, Greensboro, NC, 1987

Douglas Hofstadter, *I am a strange loop,* Basic Books, New York, 2007

Robert Kane, *A contemporary introduction to free will,* Oxford University Press, New York, 2005

Thomas R. Kelly, *A testament of devotion,* Hodder and Stoughton ., London, 1943

Arthur Koestler, *The Sleepwalkers,* Penguin, Harmondsworth, 1964

John C. Lennox, *God's undertaker: has science buried God?*, Lion Hudson, Oxford, 2007

Arnold Lloyd, *Quaker social history 1669–1738*, Longmans Green and Co., London, 1950

London Yearly Meeting during 250 years, Society of Friends, London, 1919

London Yearly Meeting Proceedings (Minutes and other documents of the Yearly Meeting; see also Britain Yearly Meeting)

Patricia Loring, *Spiritual discernment: the context and goal of clearness committees*, Pendle Hill Pamphlet 305, Pendle Hill Publications, Wallingford, PA, 1992

Patricia Loring, *Listening spirituality II: corporate spiritual practice among Friends*, Openings Press, Washington DC, 1999

Barry Morley, *Beyond Consensus: salvaging the sense of the meeting*, Pendle Hill Pamphlet 307, Pendle Hill Publications, Wallingford, PA, 1993

Nancey Murphy and George F.R. Ellis, *On the moral nature of the universe: theology, cosmology and ethics*, Fortress Press, Minneapolis, 1996

The nature and variety of concern, Quaker Home Service, London, 1986

Isaac Newton, *The Principia*, trans. Andrew Motte, Prometheus Books, Amherst, NY, 1995

Michael O'Shea, *The Brain: a very short introduction*, Oxford University Press, Oxford, 2005

Roger Penrose, *The Emperor's New Mind: concerning computers, minds and the laws of physics*, Oxford University Press, Oxford, 1989

Roger Penrose, *The road to reality: a complete guide to the laws of the universe*, Jonathan Cape, London, 2004

John Polkinghorne, *Belief in God in an age of science*, Yale University Press, New Haven and London, 1998

John C. Polkinghorne, *Science and providence: God's interaction with the world*, Templeton Foundation Press, Philadelphia and London, 2005

John Punshon, *Encounter with silence,* Friends United Press and Quaker Home Service, Richmond, IN, and London, 1987

John Punshon, *Testimony and tradition: some aspects of Quaker spirituality* (Swarthmore Lecture), Quaker Home Service, London, 1990

Quaker faith & practice, the book of Christian discipline of the Yearly Meeting of the Religious Society of Friends (Quakers) in Britain, Britain Yearly Meeting, first pubd. 1995, 3rd ed. This is the version mostly used for this book.

Matt Ridley, *The origins of virtue,* Penguin Books, London, 1997

John Robinson, *Honest to God,* SCM Press, London, 1963

Bruce Rosenblum and Fred Kuttner, *Quantum enigma,* Gerald Duckworth and Co., London, 2007

Heather Rowlands and Michael Eccles, "Discovering God in our daily life", George Gorman Lecture 2007, *Friends Quarterly,* 36-2 (2008), 22–34

Carl Sagan, *Cosmos,* Abacus, London, 1995

Janet Scott, *What canst thou say?* (Swarthmore Lecture), Quaker Home Service, London, 1980

Jackie Leach Scully, *Playing in the presence: genetics, ethics and spirituality* (Swarthmore Lecture), Quaker Books, London, 2002

John R. Searle, *The mystery of consciousness,* Granta Books, London, 1997

Michael J. Sheeran, *Beyond majority rule: voteless decisions in the Religious Society of Friends,* Philadelphia Yearly Meeting, Philadelphia, 1983

Sing in the Spirit: a book of Quaker songs, Leaveners Press, Birmingham, 2005

Pierre Teilhard de Chardin, *The phenomenon of man,* trans. Bernard Wall, William Collins, London, 1959

Anne Thomas, *Only fellow-voyagers: creation stories as guides for the journey* (Swarthmore Lecture), Quaker Home Service and Woodbrooke College, London, 1995

R.S. Thomas, *Not that he brought flowers,* Rupert Hart-Davis, London, 1955

Silvanus P. Thompson, *The quest for truth* (Swarthmore Lecture), George Allen and Unwin, London, 1915

Paul Tillich, *The shaking of the foundations,* Penguin, Harmondsworth, 1962

Keith Ward, *Pascal's fire: scientific faith and religious understanding,* Oneworld Publications, Oxford, 2006

Steven Weinberg, *The first three minutes: a modern view of the origin of the universe,* André Deutsch, London, 1977

Ken Wilber, *The marriage of sense and soul: integrating science and religion,* Random House, New York, 1998

Patricia A. Williams, *Quakerism: a theology for our time,* Infinity Publishing, West Conshohocken, PA, 2008

Bernard Wood, *Human evolution: a very short introduction,* Oxford University Press, Oxford, 2005

John Woolman, *The journal and major essays,* edited by Phillips P. Moulton, Oxford University Press, New York, 1971